D1499604

The Poetry and Poetics of Amiri Baraka

The Poetry and Poetics of
Amiri Baraka
The Jazz Aesthetic

William J. Harris

University of Missouri Press
Columbia, 1985

Library of Congress Cataloging in Publication Data

Harris, William J., 1942–
  The poetry and poetics of Amiri Baraka.

  Bibliography: p.
  Includes index.
    1. Baraka, Imamu Amiri, 1934– —Criticism and interpretation.   2. Jazz
music in literature.
3. Music and literature.   I. Title.
PS3552.A583Z68 1985   811'.54   85–1000
ISBN 0–8262–0483–X

    All passages from the works of Amiri Baraka are reproduced with the
permission of the author.
    Letters from Amiri Baraka at the Lilly Library, Indiana University, are
reproduced with the permission of Amiri Baraka and the Lilly Library.
    Citations from Richard W. Bruner's 1970 interview of Amiri Baraka are
made with the permission of Richard Bruner.
    Quotation from letter dated October 10, 1961, from Edward Dorn to Amiri
Baraka, reproduced with the permission of Edward Dorn.
    Lines from "Wichita Vortex Sutra" and "Ankor-Wat" by Allen Ginsberg
are reproduced with the permission of the Andrew Wylie Agency.
    Passages from previously unpublished letters of Charles Olson are
copyright by the Estate of Charles Olson and used with its permission.
    Lines from "I, Maximus of Gloucester, To You," from *The Maximus Poems*
by Charles Olson are reproduced with the permission of the University of
California Press and the Estate of Charles Olson.
    "Black Poet, White Critic," by Dudley Randall; "a poem to complement
other poems," by Don Lee; and "Queens of the Universe" by Sonia Sanchez
are reprinted with the permission of Dudley Randall.
    Passages from William Carlos Williams, *Pictures from Brueghel*, copyright ©
1955 by William Carlos Williams, reprinted by permission of New
Directions Publishing Corporation.

For Susan and Kate

Acknowledgments

I am indebted to a number of friends and colleagues for reading and commenting on my manuscript and to others for discussing ideas and problems related to the manuscript. It is a pleasure to give thanks to: George F. Butterick, Werner Sollors, Robert O'Meally, Charles Molesworth, Don Bialostosky, Paul Newlin, and Ruth Miller. This book could not exist without the tireless aid of Susan K. Harris.

I am grateful to Amiri Baraka for being generous with his time and for creating a major body of Afro-American literature.

I wish to thank the following libraries and individuals for permission to quote from unpublished materials: University of Connecticut Library (Storrs); George Arents Research Library, Syracuse University Library, Syracuse, New York; UCLA Library, Los Angeles, California; Lilly Library, Indiana University, Bloomington, Indiana; George Butterick for permission to quote from an undated Olson letter to Baraka and Simon Fraser University Library, Burnaby, British Columbia, Canada, for providing copies of Olson's correspondence; and Richard W. Bruner for permission to quote from his 1970 interview with Baraka, housed at The Schomburg Center for Research in Black Culture, New York, New York. In addition, James Gwynne provided me with the manuscript for Baraka's "Wise/Why's."

I also wish to express my appreciation to the Andrew W. Mellon Faculty Fellowship Program at Harvard University—especially to Rick Hunt—and to the SUNY Faculty Research Program, for their generous support.

W. J. H.
July 1985

Contents 🖋

Abbreviations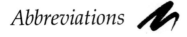

(For full citations of these works, see the Bibliography.)

A	*The Autobiography of Leroi Jones/Amiri Baraka*
AB	*Anger, and Beyond*, ed. Herbert Hill
BF	*Black Fire*
BM	*Black Music*
BMP	*Black Magic: Collected Poetry, 1961–1967*
BP	*Blues People*
C	*A Casebook on the Beat*, ed. Thomas Parkinson
DJ	*Daggers and Javelins*
DL	*The Dead Lecturer*
DS	*Dutchman and the Slave*
H	*Home: Social Essays*
HF	*Hard Facts*
"HI"	Harris, "An Interview with Amiri Baraka"
INT	*It's Nation Time*
IOT	*In Our Terribleness*
"ITT"	"In the Tradition"
J	*Jello*
M	*The Moderns*
N	*New American Poetry, 1945–1960*, ed. Donald Allen
NAS	*New American Story*, ed. Donald Allen
P	*Preface to a Twenty Volume Suicide Note*
PN	*The Poetics of the New American Poetry*, ed. Donald Allen
R	*Raise Race Rays Raze: Essays Since 1965*
RON	*Reggae or Not!*
SA	*The Sullen Art* (interview), ed. David Ossman
SD	*The System of Dante's Hell*
SP	*Selected Poetry of Amiri Baraka/LeRoi Jones*
SPP	*Selected Plays and Prose of Amiri Baraka/LeRoi Jones*
SR	*Spirit Reach*
SW	*Selected Writings* (Charles Olson)
T	*Tales*
"UW"	"Uncollected Works" (Amiri Baraka), comp. Werner Sollors

Prologue

1964

A woman asked me in all earnestness, couldn't any white help? I said, "You can help by dying. You are a cancer."—Amiri Baraka (*A*, p. 193)

April 1967

Jones sauntered on stage. He was gripping a battered orange valise, filled with manuscripts. He was a small man with a long curly beard. He wore a brown suit, an orange shirt, and an incredible green, yellow, and orange tie. "I would like to read you a couple of poems and a story . . . and talk to you," he said softly. There was a great sincerity in his voice, no rigidity, no hate. It was a loving voice. The tone said: "Brothers and sisters, I have some important things to tell you. They have to do with your survival, you hear, your survival and I love you all." Then he added in words: ". . . the colleges do not give you an education; what they give you is a training. You are trained to fit into a particular groove in white society. . . . If there is any role for the so-called educated black man, and usually what that education means is that you have been exposed more to the white disease than your brothers in the ghetto . . . it is to provide a post-American form [a black civilization]."—William J. Harris[1]

July 1967

Then another cop stepped forward. . . . "Hey, I know you," I said, just as the barrel of his .38 smashed into my forehead, dropping me into half consciousness and covering every part of me with blood. Now blows rained down on my head. One dude was beating me with the long nightstick. I was held and staggering. The blood felt hot in my face, I couldn't see, I could only feel the wet hot blood covering

---

1. William J. Harris, "Manuals for Black Militants," p. 411.

my entire head and face and hands and clothes. They were beating me to death.—Baraka (*A*, p. 262)

December 1974

Nationalism, so-called, when it says "all non-blacks are our enemies, is sickness or criminality, in fact, a form of fascism."—Baraka[2]

Midseventies

What's the answer? Revolution! Why is that? It's the only solution!
People of the world unite to defeat the two superpowers: United States imperialism, and Soviet social imperialism.
In the U.S.A., Marxist-Leninist communist party based on Marxism-Leninism-Mao Tse Tung thought!—Baraka (*DJ*, pp. 28–29)

July 1977

Well, what can I say? I know I've always tried to be a revolutionary. That's been consistent. From the time I could open my mouth in terms of talking about art I've wanted to talk about change and revolution. I think the methods and ways I've seen have changed as my own understanding has deepened. Unless something very negative happens to me, I can't see myself being anything but a revolutionary.—Baraka[3]

As an activist poet and intellectual voyager, Amiri Baraka has led a life of adventure: brutal beatings, literary successes, jail sentences, theater foundings, bohemian debaucheries, and revolutionary activities. Since Baraka has thrown himself into the social and political life of his times, he has a greater range of concrete experience to call on than many other contemporary poets. Moreover, his spiritual and intellectual adventures have kept pace with his concrete experiences; over the twenty-five-year span covered in this study he has re-created himself and his ideology several times, first as a bohemian, then as a black militant, and currently as a revolutionary socialist. Even though Baraka's biography is readily available, a review of its

2. Joseph F. Sullivan, "Baraka Abandons 'Racism,' " *The New York Times*, 27 December 1974, p. 35.
3. Tish Dace, "LeRoi Jones/Amiri Baraka," *The Village Voice*, 1 August 1977, p. 14.

highlights should help give a context for his highly autobiographical art. In addition, extant biographies need updating, and some, especially those in biographical dictionaries, need correcting.

Everett LeRoy (not LeRoi) Jones was born in the industrial city of Newark, New Jersey, on 7 October 1934. He is the son of Coyt LeRoy Jones, a retired postal supervisor, and Anna Lois Jones, a former social worker. Baraka describes his background as "middle class Negro i.e., lower middle class American" (*NAS*, p. 267). His definition of "middle class Negro" as "American" reveals his association of economics and racial integration. Not only were his parents economically upwardly mobile, but Baraka's social contacts also involved whites as well as blacks. He attended Newark's Central Avenue School, a predominantly black elementary school that nonetheless had a visible white population; a bright student, he was sent on to Barringer High School, a college prep institution from which he graduated with honors in 1951. Of his high school experience Baraka comments: "I went to a high school in New Jersey that was mainly attended by children of Italian parentage. It was 97 percent white. At first there were only six Negroes, then twelve Negroes in the entire school" (*AB*, p. 51). Perhaps one source of the adult Baraka's divided consciousness was his sense that, by excelling in the white world, he was betraying his race.

From 1952 to 1954, Baraka attended Howard University, "the capstone of Negro education," in Washington, D.C., where he studied with the famous poet-critic Sterling Brown. Because Howard refused to sanction classes that studied jazz, Brown taught Baraka, A. B. Spellman (now a major black music critic), and other interested students "something about African American music in a series of unofficial classes in the Cook Hall dormitory" (*A*, p. 74). Brown initiated Baraka into his jazz criticism by showing him that one could study black music in a serious and scholarly manner. Baraka was also instructed by a distinguished scholar of literature and religion, Nathan Scott, who introduced him to the works of Dante, later a central preoccupation in Baraka's oeuvre. In spite of these few exceptional teachers, Baraka found Howard intellectually stultifying, devoted to middle-class values and filled with Negro self-hatred. Shortly before his first year at the university, he began spelling his first name in its frenchified form, *LeRoi*. This suggests he was beginning to forge a new identity—perhaps as the "black Baudelaire"—and also suggests his sense of being of some consequence. Despite Baraka's potential, he flunked out of Howard in the fall of 1954 because he refused to conform to the university's uninspiring routines.

From 1954 to 1957, Baraka served in the United States Air Force, attaining the rank of sergeant. After basic training in Geneva, New York, he received meteorological schooling at Chanute Field in Rantoul, a town in southern Illinois. On weekends he often ventured to Chicago. Clearly, his real intellectual development began during this period. At Howard he had been a bright but unmotivated student; now, he began to write and to explore material he had ignored in school. Baraka believed his spiritual life changed dramatically one day while he looked in the window of the Green Door, a literary bookstore in Chicago:

> One time I was drifting around the South Side, near the University of Chicago, feeling alone, as usual, isolated, as usual, my usual emotional stock in trade, and I bump into this bookstore called the Green Door. It had a green door, and kind of orange plastic in the window so the sun wouldn't ruin the books. I came to rest staring into the window. There were books there I didn't recognize, a few I did. Like we'd had *Portrait of the Artist* my first year at Rutgers and I'd looked at it, but it was a *school* book and for that reason I didn't take it seriously. Though parts of it vaguely fascinated me even then. A copy of this was in the window, and next to it *Ulysses*, the book opened to the first page so you could see the words "Stately plump Buck Mulligan . . ." I stared at the words and tried to read them. I saw other books, Pound, Eliot, Thomas, philosophy books, statistics, and poetry. Something dawned on me, like a big light bulb over my noggin. The comic-strip *Idea* lit up my mind at that moment as I stared at the books. I suddenly understood that I didn't know a hell of a lot about anything. What it was that seemed to move me then was that learning was *important*. I'd never thought that before. The employment agency I'd last gone to college at, the employment agency approach of most schools I guess, does not emphasize the *beauties* the absolute *joy* of learning. . . . I vowed, right then, to learn something new every day. It was a deep revelation, something I felt throughout my whole self. I was going to learn

something every day. That's what I would do. Not just as a pas-
time, something to do in the service, but as a life commitment.
(*A*, pp. 103–4)

This story illustrates Baraka's intellectual seriousness, a trait
often overlooked by critics who concentrate on his flashier and
more provocative characteristics.

A second important insight occurred while Baraka was sta-
tioned in Puerto Rico, his first and, as it turned out, his last
permanent assignment. By then, he was seriously writing
poetry:

> I had been reading one of the carefully put together exercises
> *The New Yorker* publishes constantly as high poetic art, and grad-
> ually I could feel my eyes fill up with tears, and my cheeks were
> wet and I was crying, quietly softly but like it was the end of the
> world. . . . I was crying because I realized that I could never
> write like that writer. Not that I had any real desire to, but I
> knew even if I had had the desire I could not do it. I realized that
> there was something in me so *out*, so unconnected with what
> this writer was and what that magazine was that what was in me
> that wanted to come out as poetry could never come out like that
> and be *my* poetry. (*A*, 118)

Baraka's sense of alienation from all the *New Yorker* poem pre-
sented and represented reinforced his earlier reaction against
the traditional literature taught him at Howard. Still looking for
an alternative to establishment aesthetics, he could only per-
ceive the literary world as expressing ideals and sensibilities
that to him were remote and sterile.

In the air force, Baraka committed himself to becoming an
intellectual: reading steadily, sometimes two books a day, keep-
ing a journal, writing poetry, and submitting his poems both to
major magazines like the *New Yorker* and *Harper's* and to little
magazines as well. Given the political climate of the midfifties,
the sight of a colored man reading the *Partisan Review* in his
barracks may have been offensive. Baraka's intellectual vacation
was ended when an anonymous letter accused him of being a
communist. Although he was not political, his unorthodox li-
brary, his voracious literary appetite (he read on guard duty),
and his less than enthusiastic regard for military forms all
worked against him. In 1957 he was dishonorably discharged.

After his dismissal from the air force, Baraka settled in New York's Greenwich Village. There he became deeply involved with the entire post–World War II avant-garde. His friends and teachers included Allen Ginsberg of the Beat Generation, Frank O'Hara of the New York School, and especially Charles Olson of the Black Mountain Group, who was not only Baraka's friend, father figure, and teacher but also teacher to most of the postwar avant-garde. Olson's spirit dominated poetry in lower Manhattan even though he lived in Gloucester, Massachusetts; he was accessible on visits to New York and in his home, where Baraka visited him and corresponded with him. Baraka also corresponded about the nature of poetry and politics with Black Mountain poet Edward Dorn, who lived in Pocatello, Idaho. These poets provided the basic theory and form for all of Baraka's poetry.

In 1958, "as protection against Bohemia," Baraka married Hettie Cohen, "a middleclass Jewish lady . . . [who] produced in quick succession, two beautiful mulatto girls" (*NAS*, p. 267). Hettie was also a participant in the Beat scene, and she and Baraka co-edited the influential avant-garde literary journal *Yugen*, which published works by some of the best of the new writers, including Ginsberg, Olson, O'Hara, and Jack Kerouac. Contacts made through the magazine broadened Baraka's literary ideas and introduced him to the irregular bohemian social scene. His apartment was the site of outlandish weekend literary parties, of which he remembers:

> Poetry, literature, was our undying passion. Most of us would agree. That was the reason we all came together. But under that rubric (and defense) how many other less than kosher practices and relationships got put together? A typical weekend spontaneous bash at West 20th Street [his house] might see two or three affairs swirling around in plain view, with almost everybody in the crowd knowing what was going down, even the offended against. (*A*, p. 155)

With literature their ruling passion (or at least their common passion) members of the hip art world drifted through Baraka's apartment. Poets dropped in for days and sometimes weeks; the couch in the front room was constantly occupied. In 1959 Baraka reported to Olson: "we had a big klatch here last week . . . about

10 poets read . . . at my house . . . oppenheimer, ginsberg, blackburn, marshall, sorrentino &c. also heard dorn tapes & mcclure . . . next wk creeley tape."[4] During this time he frequented the Cedar Bar on University Place, a famous hang-out of the New York School painters and poets, and roamed Village bookstores, especially the Eighth Street and the Phoenix. He was deeply involved in the Village scene of art, ideas, drugs, and sex.

In the avant-garde, Baraka experienced a social/intellectual group whose ideas corresponded to his own. "I was drawn to them because they legitimized things I wanted to do and that I felt," he noted in an interview with D. H. Melhem.[5] For instance, Allen Ginsberg's *Howl* (1956) moved him "because it talked about a world I could identify with and relate to. His language and his rhythms were real to me. Unlike the cold edges and exclusiveness of the *New Yorker* poem that had made me cry, Ginsberg talked of a different world, one much closer to my own" (*A*, p. 150). "Allen . . . was talking about the 'nigger streets' [sic] and junkies and all kinds of things that I could see and I could identify with, and I said, yeah, that's closer to what I want to do."[6] In essence the avant-garde provided Baraka with his first intellectual and artistic models.

In 1960 Baraka visited Cuba; he has called the trip "a turning point in my life" (*A*, p. 163), noting, "Cuba split me open."[7] Visiting this new world in the Caribbean radically changed his orientation toward art and politics. After the trip he began his long voyage toward a politically committed art and, not coincidentally, a movement toward blackness and a third-world perspective. The artists he encountered in Cuba showed him the importance of politically engaged art and the egotistical irrelevance of soul-searching art, the brand he had been practicing *del norte*. His encounter with a vital and functioning revolution began the season of his discontent, a discontent that ended in

4. LeRoi Jones to Charles Olson, 26 August 1959, University of Connecticut Library (Storrs).

5. D. H. Melhem, "Revolution: The Constancy of Change: An Interview with Amiri Baraka," p. 99.

6. Ibid.

7. LeRoi Jones to Rubi (Betancourt), 1960, LeRoi Jones Collection, George Arents Research Library, Syracuse University Library.

disillusionment with his American compatriots' revolt. "The rebels," he said of his bohemian contemporaries, "have become merely people like myself who grow beards and will not participate in politics. Drugs, juvenile delinquency, complete isolation from the vapid mores of the country, a few current ways out. But name an alternative here" (*H*, p. 61). The Cuban alternative that attracted Baraka called for young intellectuals to invest their energies in creating a new and more humane society. There, in the "city of yng people," "hard yng men who know what they want" spearheaded government ministries designed to transform the social and economic nature of the society; at home, the so-called radicals of bohemia called for reform but did nothing actively, *personally*, to effect it.[8] Baraka admired the Cubans' "social radicalism," noting, "No one speaks of compromise" (*H*, p. 38).

In 1961, while he was still living in the Village, Baraka's first volume of poetry, *Preface to a Twenty Volume Suicide Note*, was published. At approximately the same time, with the poet Diane di Prima, he inaugurated the avant-garde journal *Floating Bear*, showcasing approximately the same talented coterie as *Yugen*. Out of Baraka's growing intellectual interests in black music and culture came the book *Blues People*, a profound social-aesthetic meditation on black music in particular and black art in general. In 1964 Baraka won the *Village Voice*'s Off-Broadway award, the Obie, and general critical praise for the play *Dutchman*, which brought him overnight fame. But with his sudden renown in the white world came doubts about his place in and allegiance to that world. In *The Dead Lecturer*, published in the same year but written earlier, the poet portrays his conflicting loyalties. At the jazz club the Village Vangard he complained to his old friend, the painter Larry Rivers, "Hey, you're all over in these galleries, turning out work for these rich faggots, you're part of the dying shit just like them" (*A*, p. 189). Larry Rivers, himself, comments on those days:

> LeRoi Jones, the Cisco Kid, he was a friend of mine. In the late fifties, early sixties, he was my connection to a lot of things. . . . Then after 1964, after his play *Dutchman* was produced, suddenly

8. LeRoi Jones to Hettie Cohen (1960), Arents Research Library.

it all changed. We were invited to a symposium on I don't know what—"art vs. life," some funny things—and suddenly he decided to come out of some kind of closet with the most intense hatred of every white person he knew. It was the beginning of those very aggressive situations. I couldn't believe it. I was shocked and upset, and that began the deterioration of our friendship. Finally, he told me I was just painting for a bunch of uptown fags. He's come off it a bit, like all of us do with time.[9]

His remarks to Rivers were not Baraka's only public outburst; in 1964, on another occasion at the Village Gate, when a white woman asked Baraka what whites could do to help black people, he rejoined: "You can help by dying. You are a cancer" (*A*, p. 193). His violence was a sign of his need to break with a social group that at once attracted him culturally and aesthetically and repulsed him politically.

The death of Malcolm X in 1965 was for Baraka a sign of the absolute evil of white society. He left the Village and Hettie Cohen, his personal white world, and moved uptown to Harlem, where he publicly became a cultural nationalist, committed to black people as "a race, a culture, a nation" (*H*, p. 248). Central to his break with white liberal ideology was his new assumption that blackness (race) was the most significant factor in a black person's life. Although, interestingly, his insistence that art was the best instrument for creating black culture out of the elements of black life grew out of the avant-garde aesthetics he had absorbed from that white ideology, his new goal was to incite the community to national purpose through a positive sense of black self-consciousness. With other young black intellectuals such as Larry Neal, Haki R. Madhubuti (Don L. Lee), and Ron Karenga, Baraka expanded and clarified the meaning of cultural nationalism and the Black Aesthetic. One outcome of his new goals was the founding of the Black Arts Repertory Theatre/School (BARTS) in Harlem, an influential model that inspired black theaters across the country, including Detroit, Philadelphia, Jersey City, New Orleans, and Washington, D.C. BARTS, however, had troubles with government funding (public pressures were brought to bear on the Office of Economic Op-

9. Larry Rivers, "The Cedar Bar," p. 42.

portunity's support of a "racist" project) and became caught in the political turmoils of Harlem's power structure.[10]

In all, Baraka's time in Harlem was difficult. In 1966 he returned "home," to Newark, New Jersey, where he founded Spirit House, a black repertory theater and cultural center, and married Sylvia Robinson, now known as Amina Baraka. In this same year his important book of social essays, *Home*, was published. In 1967 he assumed the Bantuized Muslim name Imamu (spiritual leader) Ameer (later Amiri, blessed) Baraka (prince), a confirmation of his blackness.[11] During the Newark riots in July 1967, Baraka was injured while being arrested on charges of unlawfully carrying weapons and resisting arrest. At his trial Judge Leon W. Kapp, of the Essex County Court, read to the all-white jury Baraka's explosive poem "Black People!" The poem included such lines as "The magic words are: Up against the wall mother / fucker this is a stick up!" Baraka's response was to demand: "I'm being sentenced for the poem. Is that what you are saying?"[12] He was convicted of a misdemeanor, sentenced to a two-year jail term, and fined one hundred dollars; his conviction was reversed on appeal. In 1969 his first book of black culturalist poetry, *Black Magic*, was published. Other works of the era were *In Our Terribleness* (1970), *It's Nation Time* (1970), and *Jello* (1970), all of which will be discussed in what follows.

Since 1974 Baraka has categorically rejected black nationalism. In a dramatic reversal of his cultural nationalist stance, Baraka published "Toward Ideological Clarity," in *Black World*, a manifesto that proclaims his conversion from black nationalism to international socialism ("Marxism-Leninism-Mao Tse Tung Thought"). As late as 1970 he had declared: "Too many radicals are so fixed on white people's philosophy, their company, their needs that they really obscure what our own people are about. We should be contemplating how to free ourselves, not trying to impose an alien philosophy on our people. . . . Our freedom

10. For a fuller account of Baraka's time in Harlem, see Theodore R. Hudson's *From LeRoi Jones to Amiri Baraka: The Literary Works*, pp. 20–25.

11. For a fuller discussion of Baraka's name, see Werner Sollors's *Amiri Baraka/LeRoi Jones: The Quest for a "Populist Modernism,"* p. 263.

12. For a more detailed review of the trial, see Hudson's *From LeRoi Jones*, pp. 29–31.

is not contained in the doctrines of Marx or Lenin."[13] But in 1974 he would say: "It is a narrow nationalism that says the white man is the enemy. . . . The black liberation movement in essence is a struggle for socialism."[14] He accounts for this radical transformation in ideology by proclaiming: "I was involved in some kind of organized political struggle that my activism caused me to continue and that continued activism is what produced my communist views. I saw that Nationalism could not solve the questions that were raised by the day by day struggle" ("HI," p. 29). For example, after his conversion to Marxism, Baraka did not feel that the election of Kenneth Gibson, a black, to the mayoralty of Newark improved the condition of black people in that city. Under neo-colonialist regimes, he contends, the color of the political figures changes but the political structure does not. Since 1974 Baraka has been committed to the creation of a "revolutionary Marxist-Leninist party" totally independent of Gus Hall's Communist party, USA. In 1975 Baraka completed his first book of Marxist poetry, *Hard Facts;* this was followed by his *Selected Poetry* (1979), which included his second and more sophisticated Marxist collection, *Poetry for the Advanced.*

In the Fall of 1979 Baraka joined the Africana Studies Department at SUNY, Stony Brook, teaching creative writing and such courses as "Great Books from the Black Experience." In the same year he was arrested in Greenwich Village after two policemen allegedly attempted to intercede in a dispute between him and his wife over the price of children's shoes. At first he was sentenced to three months on Rikers Island; however, this sentence was commuted to forty-eight consecutive weekends in a Harlem halfway house. During these weekends (1982–1983) Baraka wrote his impressive autobiography, *LeRoi Jones/Amiri Baraka* (1984).

In 1980 *The Greenfield Review* issued Baraka's long poem "In the Tradition," and the following year his *Reggae or Not* was published by Contact II Publications. Both works illustrate Baraka's development of a poetry that fuses musical with verbal forms and addresses Afro-American history. Currently, he is

13. Ida Lewis, "Conversation" (Interview with LeRoi Jones), *Essence,* September 1970, p. 25.

14. Sullivan, "Baraka," p. 35.

composing a long poem entitled "Wise/Why's" in this mode (see Appendix 2). In 1982 Baraka was tenured and promoted to associate professor at SUNY, Stony Brook. In 1984, in addition to his autobiography, his first collection of Marxist essays, *Daggers and Javelins*, was released. On 7 October 1984 Amiri Baraka celebrated his fiftieth birthday.

1. The Jazz Aesthetic

This book is about Baraka's transformations: of avant-garde poetics into ethnic poetics, of white liberal politics into black nationalist and Marxist politics, of jazz forms into literary forms. Baraka's entire career is characterized by such transformations, and I will focus on the process by which they are effected. Because it emulates a transformation process typical of jazz revision, I call Baraka's method of transformation the *jazz aesthetic,* a procedure that uses jazz variations as paradigms for the conversion of white poetic and social ideas into black ones.[1] It is important to note that the jazz aesthetic process has social as well as formal dimensions. The jazz aesthetic process, like the jazz on which Baraka draws, exists in the social world, a world where blacks are still too often second-class citizens.

1. Aesthetic here includes both a theory of beauty and a theory of action and of the political. This unorthodox definition grows out of the way critics used *aesthetic* in the expression *Black Aesthetic,* which refers to a politicized black art, a definition that is more appropriate for our purposes than the standard one, since black literature from the time of Frederick Douglass to today tends in large part to be politically engaged. Larry Neal expressed the spirit of the "Black Aesthetic" and the engaged nature of much black literature when he proclaimed, "The artist and the political activist are one" (*BF,* p. 656). The black nationalist theoretician Ron Karenga further elaborated the argument when he announced, "Black art must expose the enemy, praise the people and support the revolution" ("Black Cultural Nationalism," in *The Black Aesthetic,* ed. Addison Gayle, Jr. [Garden City: Doubleday/Anchor Press, 1972], p. 32). The "Black Aesthetic" is anti-Kantian in that the Black Aesthetician believes art should act in the world and that there are political criteria for judging art. Moreover, James T. Stewart argues, "The white Western aesthetics is predicated on the idea of separating one from the other [the social from the aesthetic]—a man's art from his actions. It is this duality that is the most distinguishable feature of Western values" (*BF,* p. 9). Stewart's simplification of the Western values aside, his statement suggests the centrality of the political to the black tradition. It is logical that the "Black Aesthetic" continues today, in at least Baraka's case, as a Marxist aesthetic since both are committed to revolutionary change. In fact, it is strange that it has taken the cultural nationalists, self-proclaimed revolutionaries, so long to come around to Marxism.

As we will see, both this jazz and the jazz aesthetic yield clues to some of the fundamental principles underlying the Afro-American response to the enveloping white world.

It must be noted that there are many moods of jazz and that Baraka's art and aesthetic grow out of one, the one that is intensely ethnic and hostile to the white world. He could have chosen a more euphoric state—say the one represented by saxophonist Lester Young or drummer Max Roach, or trumpeter Clifford Brown. Yet Baraka adopted the aggressive strain that he sees embodied especially in tenor saxophonist John Coltrane but also in such figures as singer Bessie Smith and saxophonist Charlie Parker and in such movements as bop, hard bop, and new wave. For Baraka the essence of this tradition can be characterized as saying to the white world: "Kiss my ass, kiss my black unruly ass" (*DS*, p. 35).

In 1965, commenting on Coltrane's work, Baraka declared: "Trane is a mature swan whose wing span was a whole world. But he also shows us how to murder the popular song. To do away with weak Western forms. He is a beautiful philosopher" (*BM*, p. 174). For Baraka, Coltrane epitomizes the jazz aesthetic process: he is the destroyer of Western forms. For example, in "Nature Boy" from *The John Coltrane Quartet Plays Chim Chim Chere . . .* Coltrane takes a weak Western form, a popular song, and murders it; that is, he mutilates and disembowels this shallow but bouncy tune by using discordant and aggressive sounds to attack and destroy the melody line. The angry black music devours and vomits up the fragments of the white corpse. For Baraka, Coltrane is a beautiful philosopher because he ventured to shatter and twist and finally eradicate Western structures. Baraka says of Coltrane's destructive art, "He'd play sometimes chorus after chorus, taking the music apart before our ears, splintering the chords and sounding each note, resounding it, playing it backwards and upside down trying to get to something else. And we heard our own search and travails, our own reaching for new definition. Trane was our flag" (*A*, p. 176). By playing the notes backwards and upside down Coltrane was searching for a new non-Western self among the rubble of Western forms, a new arrangement of notes that would be the source for a new definition of reality and ethnic identity. Among these fragments Coltrane sought to structure a new black world.

Baraka also wants to take weak Western forms, rip them asunder, and create something new out of rubble. He transposes Coltrane's musical ideas to poetry, using them to turn white poetic forms backwards and upside down. This murderous impulse is behind all the forms of Baraka's aesthetic and art. In his current Marxist stage, this deadly impulse is directed not merely against the white world per se but also against the capitalists who Baraka credits with creating racism. This study embraces the term *jazz aesthetic* to describe the mode that will free Baraka from the artistic and metaphysical domination of the white world.

Henry Louis Gates's discussion of formal revision or parody in the black literary tradition will help us further clarify the jazz aesthetic process. He presents one principal formula of the murderous impulse when he explains that the mode

> suggests a given structure precisely by failing to coincide with it—that is, suggests it by dissemblance. Repeating a form and then inverting it through a process of variation is central to jazz—a stellar example is John Coltrane's rendition of "My Favorite Things," compared to Julie Andrews' vapid version.[2]

Gates, then, finds that the chief means by which jazz creates a transformation is by repeating, and then inverting. Of course this pattern is not unique to jazz; rather it is a general description of parody. Yet, even though repetition and inversion are not peculiar to jazz, they are specific to it, forming the prevalent pattern underlying jazz compositions. Moreover, what is unique to jazz is the particular style (emphasis on rhythm, on fusion of voice and instrument, and a digression from the Western scale into the blues scale of "bent tones," flatted thirds and sevenths); the general musical conception of revision (the spontaneous revision of preexisting themes into a new idiom); the unique indigenous parodic model that jazz makes available; and the particular American racial situation to which the parody is responding. Jazz musicians like Coltrane have routinely revised popular white tunes into black compositions by criticizing and parodying white songs; their listeners can identify the original song but sense that it has been altered to fit a different perspec-

2. "The 'Blackness of Blackness': A Critique of the Sign and the Signifying Monkey," pp. 693–94.

tive. Baraka's application of this inversion formula from jazz to black art and black life is not the only formulation of the jazz aggressive impulse, but it is a formulation that is central to Baraka's art, an art that constantly changes existent tropes, ideas, symbols, images, and social forms from white to black. The formula can express itself in various forms of destruction from inversion to mutilation. In his constant desire to smash prevailing forms, a tendency that in large part grows out of his blackness, Baraka is one of contemporary America's most radical and innovative artists.

When Gates focuses on inversion in black literature, he sees black writers turning their black predecessors upside down: he discusses Ralph Ellison's revisions of Richard Wright, and Ishmael Reed's of both Wright and Ellison. Baraka, too, revises his "fathers," but rather than looking to his black predecessors Baraka looks to his white ones: to Ezra Pound, to William Carlos Williams, to Charles Olson, and to Allen Ginsberg. Like Coltrane, he transforms white forms and ideas into black ones through a jazz process; his poetry reveals his attraction to his white fathers' ideas, his battles with them, his rejection of them, and, finally, his transformation of them into his own rich and multifarious black art.

It is not surprising that black music should provide the paradigm for Baraka's art. Early in his career he found it the highest achievement of black culture. In 1966 he commented, "Only in music, and most notably in blues, jazz, and spirituals, i.e., 'Negro Music,' has there been a significantly profound contribution by American Negroes" (*H*, p. 106). He had discovered the music as a teenager in Newark; he encountered white avant-garde art when he came to the Village as a young man in his twenties. Yet the attraction of bohemian art was in part the characteristics it shared with black music: both protested the dominant culture by inverting dominant forms. The bohemian inverted bourgeois forms, and the jazz musician inverted white ones—both wanted to turn the entrenched world upside down. In both cases the inversion had a social source. The bohemian wanted to invert what he felt was a hypocritical and repressive world, and the black wanted to invert what he thought of as a racist and oppressive world. Although Baraka at first saw these two inversions as identical, in time he decided that the avant-garde inversion was not adequate to meet his needs as a black artist and activist: "Laying up and getting high" did not produce real inversions. Finally, he turned to third-world Marxist inversions—revolutions—to find a process that reflected the inversions of black music.

From the white avant-garde Baraka learned how to write and think about poetry, but from jazz he learned how to reject, invert, and transform what the white avant-garde had taught him. For instance, Baraka takes William Carlos Williams's method of writing verse in the American idiom and repeats it. That is, Baraka writes verse first in the white colloquial language that he, like Williams, learned growing up in New Jersey, and then he repeats it in an Afro-American transformation of the American idiom that is more capable of reflecting the rhythms of black life and speech. Similarly, Allen Ginsberg found Williams a model for the American vernacular and in his early poetry, *Empty Mirror* (written between 1947 and 1953, published in 1961),[3] imitated Williams. For Ginsberg, too, the later, mature poetry grew out of the sounds of his own experience—the voices of his generation and of his Jewish context. Yet Ginsberg's transformations are not motivated by an ethnic adversarial imperative; his argument with America seems to be more political than ethnic.

Baraka's changes are unique among the contemporary avant-garde because he is consciously transforming white forms into black ones, consciously choosing a method that grows out of a black tradition, because for him, finally, avant-garde forms were not enough. Despite a strong identification with the bohemian poets, he had to face the realities of being black in America, and in America simply adding the adjective *black* transforms a concept. To couple the word *black* to an idea makes it dangerous and alien to many white people; conversely, it makes it affirming and communal to many black people. Consequently, Baraka felt obliged to turn the ideas and the forms of avant-garde art into black art, taking the avant-garde didactic and turning it into black didactic, white dada into black dada, avant-garde critiques of the West into black critiques, and avant-garde stereotypes of blacks into revolutionary black images for blacks. It is important

3. Thomas F. Merrill, *Allen Ginsberg* (New York: Twayne Publishers, 1969), p. 64.

to realize that Baraka's current Marxist revolutionary national-
ism both extends and negates his cultural nationalism. He is
still committed to revolutionary revolt, but it is now defined in
Marxist terms; the enemy is no longer the white man, but the
capitalist state. Nevertheless, he still generally identifies the
capitalist as white. Marxism has not destroyed Baraka's belief in
the autonomous black state and the uniqueness of black culture;
it has only given him a framework for seeing the black struggle
for independence in economic and materialist terms. Currently,
Lenin, Stalin, and Wright help define the national question for
him instead of Karenga and Madhubuti. But Baraka is not sim-
ply a Marxist, he is a third-world Marxist—race as well as eco-
nomics is a factor in his revolutionary ideology. Baraka never
rejects his central cultural nationalist statement that "Black Peo-
ple are a race, a culture, a Nation" (*H*, p. 248): he continues to
find black culture a source of vitality and wisdom—of psychic
health. Therefore, his shift from cultural nationalist to revolu-
tionary Marxist was not as abrupt as it has often been seen: he
has carried over the most revolutionary elements of his cultural
nationalism into his Marxism. In borrowing as in transforming,
Baraka continues to draw, whether consciously or uncon-
sciously, on what at an early stage of his career he called the
highest achievements of Western culture: jazz and white avant-
garde art and thought. Throughout his career, even during the
current Marxist stage, he has used the jazz aesthetic process to
create a new black art from the artistic and conceptual innova-
tions of the twentieth-century avant-garde.

Baraka's transformations are not always neatly expressed in
terms of symmetrical inversions or formal assassinations; rather
(once again like jazz) his creative destructions take many forms:
rejection, extremism/completion, violence, dismemberment,
creative anger, and revolution. These seemingly disparate terms
are all variations of the same aesthetic impulse, an impulse ex-
pressed in a black music often far ahead of black literature in its
complex fusions of love and hate, creation and destruction. Fi-
nally, even though the jazz aesthetic is peculiar to black life in
that both the process and the style of transformation grow out
of the particulars of the black experience, it is nevertheless a
specific response to the universal problem of social and cultural
domination.

Even though they do not use the terms, both Houston Baker and William C. Fischer have also observed the workings of the jazz process in Baraka's poetry. In an important essay, Baker argues, "Baraka . . . inverts the literary-critical optimism and axiology of an earlier generation, rejecting entirely the notion that 'Negro Literature' should not stand apart as a unique body of expression."[4] Despite his apparent lack of awareness of a general procedure of inversion in Baraka's work, Baker finds it appropriate to describe Baraka's generational struggle in terms of reversal, even when speaking of Baraka's relationship with black, rather than white, predecessors. Similarly, Fischer, one of the best critics of Baraka, is aware of inversion as an ongoing process in Baraka's work. Speaking of symbol inversion in the early poem "Hymn for Lanie Poo," he notes: "By inverting this traditional life-giving symbol [the sun], Jones practices a strategy common to the black perspective: reversing the destructive meanings and values projected by the white world in order to buffer the besieged black psyche."[5] Fischer rightly connects Baraka's poetic technique with the black perspective, the black Weltanschauung—a relationship I will discuss in some detail later. Neither critic, however, has fully sensed the jazz aesthetic process in its totality—they observe aspects of it in isolation without identifying them as parts of a larger process. Furthermore, neither critic discusses the centrality of this process to Baraka's entire career, that is, that it can be regarded as the main organizing principle of his poetics and that it has its source in the aggressive and anti-assimilationist elements of black music.

Jazz is an ideal paradigm for criticizing and parodying the white tradition because it is a "signifying" tradition. The linguist Geneva Smitherman has defined signification, a mode of black discourse, as "the verbal art of insult in which a speaker humorously puts down, talks about, needles—that is, signifies on—the listener."[6] Coltrane is signifying on the white song when he rearranges it; he mocks and parodies the sentimental-

4. Houston A. Baker, "Generational Shifts and the Recent Criticism of Afro-American Literature," p. 5.

5. William C. Fischer, "Amiri Baraka," in *American Writers* (suppl. 2, pt. 1), ed. A. Walton Litz, p. 31.

6. *Talkin and Testifyin*, p. 118.

ity of the Julie Andrews rendition. In the short story "A Coupla Scalped Indians," Ralph Ellison illustrates jazz signification when he has one of his main characters interpret black music to his friend:

> "How about that trumpet?"
> "Him? That fool's a soldier, he's really signifying,
> Saying,
>> 'So ya'll don't play 'em, hey?
>> So ya'll *won't* play 'em, hey?
>> Well pat your feet and clap your hands,
>> 'Cause I'm going to play 'em to the promised
>> land . . ."
> "Man, if the white folks know what that fool is signifying on that horn they'd run him clear on out the world. Trumpet's got a real *nasty* mouth."
> "Why you call him a soldier, man?" I said.
> "'Cause he's slipping 'em in the twelves and choosing 'em, all at the same time. Talking 'bout they mamas and offering to fight 'em. Now he ain't like that ole clarinet; clarinet so sweet-talking he just eases you in the dozens."[7]

The dozens is a form of signification. Smitherman says of it: "What you do in playing the Dozens is sig on a person's kinfolk—usually the mother, the closest kin—instead of siggin on the person. The player can extend the put-down, by analogy, to include other immediate relatives, and even ancestral kinfolk."[8] Like Ellison's trumpeter, Baraka is a soldier who is willing to fight; he does not, like the clarinet player, sweeten the sound of his instrument. And the dozens he played until he became a Marxist was played on the whole Western tradition, on the "ancestral kinfolk" of the white traditions he tries to reject. Like Ishmael Reed, who—especially in *Mumbo Jumbo*—also signifies on the white Western ancestor worship, Baraka refuses to accept the notion that the West is best. With the transformations afforded him by the jazz aesthetic process, Baraka plays the dozens in a variety of poems, including "Word from the Right Wing" ("President Johnson / is a mass murderer, and his mother, was a mass murderer, / and his wife / is weird looking, a special breed / of hawkbill cracker" [*BMP*, p. 93]). In play-

---

7. Ralph Ellison, "A Coupla Scalped Indians," p. 230.
8. *Talkin*, p. 131.

ing the dozens on America's prominent men, he continues his antagonistic stance and lays the ground for future transformations.

One way to begin examining Baraka's transformations is to note how often the concept of turning—even the verb *to turn*—occurs in his work. In his discussion of the revolutionary minstrels in his play *The Slave* (1964), he provides a clear illustration of the inversion process:

> I think one interesting thing in *The Slave* is that I had the army, Walker Vessels' army, wear revolutionary patches with minstrels on them. Grinning minstrels. What that meant to me was that would turn that very symbol for blacks into something of terror for whites. The grinning Uncle Sambo with red lips and the white teeth would strike fear in their hearts . . . would make revolution. ("HI," p. 25)

The "turning" Baraka refers to here involves taking a white stereotype of blacks, the grinning minstrel, and transforming it into a symbol of its opposite, the militant revolutionary.

Claiming, "The largest work of art is the world itself" (*R*, p. 129), Baraka extends jazz inversion beyond tropes to social systems, making it a revolutionary process politically as well as formally. Thus Baraka's repetitions broadened in scope as he matured, a process that can be traced through his various stages: during his early Beat years he repeated avant-garde forms without parodying them, thus producing Beat poems; in his transitional stages from Beat to black allegiances, he repeated avant-garde forms but also parodied them, producing a critique of the white avant-garde; and after he became a cultural nationalist and even after he became a revolutionary nationalist, he repeated the elements from the white avant-garde tradition that he found useful for black poetry, exaggerating and completing them, using them as the basis for a new tradition. In all these repetitions the models lay in black music. For the black poet, the jazz artist is an exemplar because he is involved in the act of creative destruction: in his apocalyptic art, endings open out to new beginnings.

As we have already noted, Baraka encountered the white avant-garde when he came to Greenwich Village as a young man. From the late 1950s through the mid-1960s he was a central figure of the Village scene, publishing avant-garde magazines such as *Yugen* and *Floating Bear*, hanging out in bohemian night spots like the White Horse Tavern and the Cedar Bar, and opening his house to avant-garde poets, poetry readings, and parties. He was, in fact, totally immersed, both personally and artistically, in that bohemian world. There he was influenced not only by the contemporary avant-garde—especially Charles Olson and Allen Ginsberg—but also by their "spiritual Fathers," the pre–World War I modernists, especially Ezra Pound and William Carlos Williams.

In discussing Baraka's revisions of twentieth-century avant-garde ideas I am, of course, implying a theory of literary influence; clearly, his art did not spring fully formed and new as if from Zeus's forehead. Rather, like all original thought, Baraka's is a process of transformation. One motivation for replacing old forms with new—certainly a motivation in the black artistic community—is ideological; sons transform their fathers' values. Ralph Ellison, discussing Richard Wright, one of his own literary fathers, notes,

> I felt no need to attack what I considered the limitations of Wright's vision because I was quite impressed by what he had achieved. And in this, although I saw with the black vision of Ham, I was, I suppose, as pious as Shem and Japheth. Still, I would write my own books and they would be in themselves, implicitly, criticisms of Wright's; just as all novels of a given historical moment form an argument over the nature of reality and are, to an extent, criticism of each other.[9]

As Ellison clearly sensed, by its nature the revision process builds on the works of strong or prior authors—authors who have created a vision of reality with which the younger author must contend before he can define himself. Ellison's writings are a critique of Wright's because they question Wright's concept of the nature of reality. Similarly, Baraka's poems since 1964 criticize white avant-garde visions of reality. Both authors must overcome their predecessors; they must, as Harold Bloom says, "clear imaginative space for themselves."[10] In rewriting white

9. *Shadow and Act*, p. 124.
10. *The Anxiety of Influence*, p. 5.

texts, in criticizing white visions of reality, Baraka creates a new vision that fuses the forms and ideas he learned from others with the realities of his experience as a black man in America.

Understanding the jazz aesthetic is crucial to understanding Baraka's poetry because it provides the means through which this fusion is effected. The jazz aesthetic, having its source in the radical and aggressive musical tradition of Parker and Coltrane, is itself a critique of white America. In 1966 Baraka commented on this implicit reversal when he noted, "The song title 'A White Man's Heaven is a Black Man's Hell' describes how complete an image reversal is necessary in the West" (*H*, p. 247). Here, the song title suggests that the black's misery is a consequence of the white man's comfort, his dependence on the service of the black masses. Clearly, one reason the jazz aesthetic is important to Baraka is that its roots are in such social and economic realities. In Baraka's work the implicit ideology of the jazz aesthetic becomes explicit.

In addition, the linguistic habits of blacks reflect the need for image reversals: the inverting of white words to render black meanings comments on the antagonism and mistrust blacks feel toward whites. For example, in the black oral lexicon *bad* means *good* because it means *bad* in the white lexicon. Baraka extends this linguistic habit by pushing it to its extreme—a form of the jazz process that I call *extremism*. Baraka intensifies *bad* into *terrible* and creates a new black art form: *bad* is black speech; *terrible* is black poetry.

> Our terribleness is our survival as
> beautiful beings, any where.
> Who can dig that?
> To be bad is one level
> But to be terrible, is to be
> badder dan nat   (*IOT*, unpaginated)

For Baraka as for other black artists, blacks can only escape the white hell through a radical transformation of white images, ideas, and forms. Here, to be terrible is to be extreme, one way of radically confronting that hell. By becoming the white man's idea of terrible, the black man assumes stature and becomes, in his own eyes, strong and beautiful. In Baraka's poem from *In*

Our Terribleness (1970), to be terrible is to exist, to confront, and implicitly to terrify: all radical alternatives to the invisibility of the white man's ideal black.

That the inversion process has operated in black value systems for a long time is evident in a passage from Booker T. Washington's classic *Up from Slavery* (1901):

> At the time I went to Alabama the coloured people were taking considerable interest in politics, and they were very anxious that I should become one of them politically, in every respect. They seemed to have a little distrust of strangers in this regard. I recall that one man, who seemed to have been designated by the others to look after my political destiny, came to me on several occasions and said, with a good deal of earnestness: "We wants you to be sure to vote jes' like we votes. We can't read de newspapers very much, but we knows how to vote, an' we wants you to vote jes' like we votes." He added: "We watches de white man, and we keeps watching de white man till we finds out which way de white man's gwine to vote; an' when we finds out which way de white man's gwine vote den we votes 'xactly de other way. Den we know we's right."[11]

This anecdote demonstrates the political implications of the jazz aesthetic process. These semiliterate blacks vote "'xactly de other way" to counter the white vote, which they cannot imagine could be in their interest. Washington's story tells much about blacks' perceptions of whites and embodies the same message as the song title "A White Man's Heaven Is a Black Man's Hell." The impulse to invert the desperate conditions of black life is reflected in the formal inversions of black language, black art, and even black politics. The jazz aesthetic process is a particular formula that has its source in that life and is reflected in black art.

Baraka's transformations encompass not only processes but images as well. As a black artist, he is obsessed with white images because they create and control the nature of reality for both whites and blacks. In the early book of essays, *Home*, he asserts:

> What a culture produces, is, and refers to, is an image—a picture of a process, since it is a form of a process: movement seen. . . .

11. *Up from Slavery* in *Three Negro Classics*, intro. John Hope Franklin (New York: Avon Books, 1965), p. 88.

Good-Bad, Beautiful-Ugly, are all formed as the result of image. The mores, customs, of a place are the result of experience, and a common reference for defining it—common images. . . . The various black porters, gigglers, ghostchumps and punkish Indians, etc., that inhabit the public image the white man has fashioned to characterize Black Men in the West, since that's what is run on them each day by white magic, i.e., television, movies, radio, etc.—the Mass Media (the *Daily News* does it with flicks and adjectives). (*H*, p. 247)

Through the mass media, white culture has created images of blacks that are inherently embedded in the culture's definitional dualities; to survive, black artists must create counter images of their own. That is, because white culture has placed blacks on the dark end of its dualities—they are the evil in good/evil, the ugly in beautiful/ugly—the duty, the imperative, of Baraka's ideal black artist is to destroy those dualities or, at least, to establish counter dualities that will appeal as strongly, as magically, to consciousness as the white images. This "black magic" is a weapon in the war for black minds.

Again, Baraka's theory that the mass media are responsible for controlling the images all Americans have of black people is a variant of several contemporary critiques of mind control, especially among white avant-garde writers like William Burroughs and Allen Ginsberg. Ginsberg contends:

Recent history is the record of a vast conspiracy to impose one level of mechanical consciousness on mankind and exterminate all manifestations of the unique part of human sentience, identical in all men, which the individual shares with his Creator. The suppression of contemplative individuality is nearly complete.

The only immediate historical data that we can know and act on are those fed to our senses through systems of mass communication.

These media are exactly the places where the deepest and most personal sensitivities and confessions of reality are most prohibited, mocked, suppressed. (*C*, p. 25)

Both Ginsberg and Baraka criticize the mass media for controlling access to information and, more importantly, for their power to implant images in the preconscious psyche. But Baraka's concern takes a form radically different from Ginsberg's.

While the white American writer fears the power of the media to harness the individual spirit, the black American fears its power to paralyze the spirit of his people. Baraka's commitments are collective; Ginsberg's are to the unfettered soul. Thus, while Ginsberg's politics spring from Emersonian individualism, Baraka's spring from ethnic collectivism. But Baraka, too, echoes Emerson—and Whitman—when he argues that the function of the black artist is to shape consciousness: "The Black artist . . . is desperately needed to change the images his people identify with, by asserting Black feeling, Black mind, Black judgment" (*H*, p. 248).

As he changed from a Beat artist to a cultural nationalist one, Baraka's goal was to achieve "racial integrity" for the black citizen; that is, to destroy the citizen's old images of himself and implant new ones; although his current Marxism calls for broader racial relationships, he still believes in black leaders (including black artists) for black people. As the jazz artist presents, destroys, and re-creates the musical modes with which he begins, so the poet presents, counters, and re-creates the images that are presented by the dominant culture. Baraka critic Kimberly W. Benston has noted, "As trumpeter Clifford Thronton (alumnus of the fabulous Sun Ra cabal) declared, true revolution of consciousness begins by a radical 'un-learning' of existent modes. It is not an improvement or modification of available techniques that the black artist requests; rather, his call is for an entirely new grammar, a 'post Western form' (Baraka et al.)."[12]

Another way to look at the destructive, or unlearning, process that is part of the black artistic response to white forms and ideas is to see it as a form of parricide. In recent years Harold Bloom and his disciples have expanded the notion of parricide into the realm of literary influence. Like parricide, Baraka's transformation of Western forms alters a repressive relationship, it is a symbolic murder of domineering literary fathers. With other minority artists, Baraka is engaged in a battle with his literary predecessors—not just with the immediate ones but with the whole tradition of white European and American literature—that is a necessary prelude to the development of his

12. "Late Coltrane: A Re-membering of Orpheus," in *Chant of Saints*, ed. Michael S. Harper, pp. 414–15.

own sense of authority and his own distinctive voice. But minority parricides take on aspects that are indigenous to the culture from which the parricidal processes spring. Ellison, for instance, in the opening pages of *Invisible Man* (1952), retells the primordial parricide in terms of Afro-American myth and history. In his version, a horde of mulatto sons seeks to kill a primal father who is not only their biological father but also their slave master. The mother, caught between her love for her master/ lover and her desire for freedom for herself and her sons, poisons the man whose existence has at once given life to her sons and absolutely determined the forms their lives would take. Here, a primal tale—a universal experience of the need for rebellion—is embodied in particulars that are group specific.

In addition, the particulars of this situation logically lead to violence, either physical, political, or psychological. For Eldridge Cleaver the violence was physical: "subjected people," he declares, "have a desire to kill their masters."[13] Norman O. Brown sees it in political, Freudian-Lockean terms (rather than, as minority artists often see it, in a Marxist paradigm): "The primal father is absolute monarch of the horde. . . . The sons form a conspiracy to overthrow the despot, and in the end substitute a social contract with equal rights for all."[14] In the poem "Black Dada Nihilismus," in order to free himself from their power and influence, Baraka summons up the demon of blackness to "choke my [white] friends" (*DL*, p. 63)—to kill his white friends who happened to be also his fathers (not only was he the youngest chronologically, he also placed himself in a filial position when he came to the Village to "learn how" to rebel against the middle class). The difference between Cleaver, Brown, and Baraka is the difference between physical, political, and psychological parricide: Cleaver, responding to a short-lived revolutionary climate, suggests that the masters must be really killed; Brown displaces the inherent violence of his paradigm onto the vagaries of political myth; while Baraka suggests that the parricide is of the person of the father absorbed in the sons, that is, of the white images that blacks, especially one young black poet, have absorbed through their immersion in the

13. "Psychology: The Black Bible," in *New Black Voices,* ed. Abraham Chapman (New York: New American Library, 1972), p. 475.
14. *Love's Body* (New York: Random House, 1966), p. 3.

dominant culture. While Baraka's poem is about freeing the black masses from the shackles of white images, it is also about freeing himself from the images, forms, and ideologies that he learned from his avant-garde friends.

Certainly black artists are not the only group to express a parricidal impulse prior to the development of their own voices. Much minority art is art of creative anger. The dissenting poet William Blake—a minority of one—knew that violence and anger are necessary for the artist's release from his old value systems: in "The Marriage of Heaven and Hell" (1793) he asserts, "The tygers of wrath are wiser than the horses of instruction."[15] More explicitly, Blake states in *Jerusalem:* "I must create a system or be enslaved by another Man's."[16] More recently, women have expressed the need to rid themselves violently of self-images implanted by a patriarchal culture. Adrienne Rich rages against the "world masculinity made / unfit for women or men," and she seeks to create a new world free of male domination.[17] Similarly, in "A Poem for Black Hearts" Baraka demands revenge on the white world for the death of Malcolm X:

> For Great Malcolm a prince of the earth, let nothing
>   in us rest
> until we avenge ourselves for his death, stupid animals
> that killed him, let us never breathe a pure breath if
> we fail, and white men call us faggots till the end of
> the earth.   (*BMP*, p. 112)

Frantz Fanon's and Jean Paul Sartre's discussions of cleansing anger, which, like Cleaver's ideology, sprang from the political climate of the 1960s, are still pertinent for minority artists. Fanon asserts: "At the level of individuals, violence is a cleansing force. It frees the native from his inferiority complex and from his despair and inaction; it makes him fearless and restores his self-respect."[18] Sartre, commenting on Fanon, precisely assesses Fanon's conception of therapeutic violence:

15. *The Complete Poetry and Selected Prose of John Donne and The Complete Poetry of William Blake,* intro. Robert Silliman Hillyer (New York: Random House, 1941), p. 654.

16. Ibid., p. 902.

17. Adrienne Rich, *Diving into the Wreck* (New York: Norton, 1973), p. 36.

18. *The Wretched of the Earth,* p. 73.

> They [white Europeans] would do well to read Fanon; for he shows clearly that this irrepressible violence is neither sound and fury, nor the resurrection of savage instincts, nor even the effect of resentment: it is man re-creating himself. I think we understood this truth at one time, but we have forgotten it—that no gentleness can efface the marks of violence; only violence itself can destroy them. The native cures himself of colonial neurosis by thrusting out the settler through force of arms. When his rage boils over, he rediscovers his lost innocence and he comes to know himself in that he himself creates his self.[19]

Like the native, the minority artist engages in a violent struggle; his, however, is with words, and his creation is a new culture. Clearly, a similar aesthetic evolves in any situation in which the artist feels himself to be in an inferior position to the dominant culture. The specific formula for an individual artist's struggle, however, grows out of the particulars of his or her given social and cultural situation, and these are the particulars that make his or her creations unique. As Baraka himself notes, "For every culture there is a definite set of aesthetic, moral, etc., judgments based quite literally on specifically indigenous emotional and psychological response" (*H*, p. 131).

Baraka's most radical move, from being an apolitical Beatnik to being a politically engaged cultural nationalist, provides an important example of how the jazz aesthetic process embodies forms for social as well as artistic change. His cultural nationalist poetry not only describes change but also calls for it; in this phase of his career, Baraka says: "We want 'poems that kill' " (*BMP*, p. 116). Like Rich, Baraka is parricidal because he wants to make room for himself; both poets espouse the concept of violent change because only after a revolution of values will their own voices be heard. For Baraka, effecting these changes is a dangerous political act, one to which Malcolm X was a martyr:

> For Malcolm's words
> fire darts, the victor's tireless
> thrusts, words hung above the world
> change as it may, he said it, and
> for this he was killed, for saying,
> and feeling, and being/change   (*BMP*, p. 112)

19. "Preface" to *Wretched of the Earth*, p. 18.

Even Baraka's Marxism embodies the dual notion of social and psychological change. Like the verb *to turn* mentioned earlier, the verb *to change* bears great significance in his poetry. In the Marxist poem "When We'll Worship Jesus" he asserts:

> we can change the world
> we can struggle against the forces of backwardness,
> we can change the world
> we can struggle against our selves, our slowness   (*HF*, p. 8)

Baraka's Marxism is only another phase of his transformations, of the interchange between verbal and social forms. The "forces of backwardness" are as much internal as external, they are states of mind as well as social systems.

While Baraka's need to destroy his literary predecessors is shared by other minority artists, his particular relationship with his fathers is unusual and complex.[20] Unlike the entrenched patriarchal culture against which Rich struggles, or the French cultural establishment that Fanon fought, Baraka's fathers are rebels. Ginsberg and Olson, Pound and Williams, the white avant-garde of both generations, were themselves involved in the process of overthrowing their fathers. Baraka was originally drawn to them precisely because they inverted white middle-class values and seemed to promise an escape from the bourgeois culture he rejected. But the white avant-garde did not, finally, go far enough. As we shall see, its establishment of counter forms was not complete enough for the black artist, and his rejection of the avant-garde artists was as profound—and as painful—as their rejection of their own fathers. But, paradoxically, rejecting the white avant-garde artists was also to be true to them; turning their weapons against them was still to use the weapons they gave him. In turning from bohemianism to black-

20. See Frantz Fanon's three stages of the native writer for interesting parallels with Baraka's development. Even though in his first stage Fanon is too categoric about assimilation, lumping all foreign influences together, the second stage, where the alienated native wants to return to his culture, is very similar to Baraka's cultural nationalist period, and the third stage, where the native wants to awaken the people, is analogous to both Baraka's nationalist and Marxist periods. Yet one serious shortcoming of the paradigm is that it does not take into consideration the absorption of rebellious elements from the dominant culture by certain native artists. *Wretched of the Earth*, pp. 178–79.

ness, Baraka showed himself to be his rejected fathers' heir. Similarly, Baraka's relationship with Marx in his revolutionary nationalist stage bears the same impulse for completion and extremism; he comes to Marx through Mao, a political ideologue with a third-world sensibility. In espousing Mao's brand of communism, Baraka expands the white European model to cover both nonwhite and non-European people.

Jean Paul Sartre points to a similar situation in his discussion of the French surrealists and the Martinique surrealist Aimé Césaire. "In Césaire, the great surrealist tradition is realized, it takes on its definitive meaning and is destroyed: surrealism— that European movement—is taken from the Europeans by a Black man who turns it against them and gives it a rigorously defined function."[21] In the end, Baraka and Césaire are literary terrorists, destroyers of established institutions, not bohemians. Both perceive strains of anarchy, violence, and self-hatred in the white avant-garde tradition—the anarchism of dada-surrealism, for instance, or the rejection of the West that led Gauguin and D. H. Lawrence to embrace alien and exotic cultures. Moreover, the gun that André Breton dreams of shooting off, randomly, in the street, Césaire and Baraka aim at specific institutions that they see as embodiments of Western culture. With their "sociocultural aesthetic" they want to change not only psychic structures (consciousness) but also political structures (governments); they want their poetry to create revolt in the streets. Moreover, although Baraka switched from espousing spontaneous to espousing organized revolt as he moved from being a black nationalist to being a third-world Marxist, his commitment to the principle of revolution remained unchanged.

In jazz aesthetic fashion, Baraka's and Césaire's extremism leads to completion, that is, to the full realization of the original avant-garde idea. Thus the avant-garde ideology, when realized by the black extremist, contains the seeds of its own destruction. The black avant-garde artist realizes his white counterparts' ideology, embracing destruction with delight and using it to wreck the white tradition. To destroy the dominating tradition is to give the black the possibility of finding his own sense

---

21. "Black Orpheus," in *The Black American Writer,* ed. C. W. E. Bigsby, 2:23.

of self and tradition. Therefore the black bohemian artist will not settle for a mere "rearrangement of reality" but seeks the "creation of a new reality after the destruction of the old" (*DJ*, p. 200). He does not want to shock the bourgeoisie; he wants to destroy it. For instance, when Allen Ginsberg approvingly describes a character in "Howl" (1956) throwing "potato salad at CCNY lecturers on Dadaism"[22] as a true act of Dada, he is condoning a mild form of havoc in bourgeois society; but when Baraka uses dada in such poems as "Black Dada Nihilismus," he is trying to marshal the irrational forces of dada ("Come up, black dada / nihilismus. Rape the white girls. Rape / their fathers" [*DL*, p. 63]) to bring an end to white civilization. Baraka says of the third-world surrealists: "The surrealism Senghor and Césaire asked for from the French Negro poets was a more dramatically African use of French, which they thought should be in defiance of European rationalism and not merely thin replicas of Breton or Tzara" (*H*, p. 131). Moreover in *The Autobiography* (1984) Baraka compares his work with Césaire's:

> I was tearing away from the "ready-mades" that imitating Creeley (or Olson) provided. . . . So I scrambled, and roamed, sometimes, blindly in my consciousness, to come up with something more essential, more rooted in my deepest experience. . . . It was almost like what Césaire had said about how he wrote *Return to My Native Land*. That he was trying to break away from the heavy influence that French Symbolist poetry [*sic*] had on him. So he decided to write prose to stop writing poetry. . . . showing how even the French language could be transformed by the Afro-Caribbean rhythms and perceptions. (p. 166)

In Baraka's analysis of Césaire, the third-world poet turns to the dada technique to free himself from the domination of white Western language. But in Baraka's own work this process extends to the destruction of Western forms and ideas as well.

Baraka conceives of jazz and dada-surrealism as analogues since he finds the inversion process central to both. In his *Autobiography* he says of the surrealists: "The shit had to be turned upside down" (*A*, p. 159). In fact, there are striking similarities between Sartre on surrealism and Baraka on jazz:

22. *Howl and Other Poems*, p. 15.

In jazz, people started talking about "funk," and the white man had always said: "The Negro has a characteristic smell," but then the Negro takes that and turns the term around, so that if you don't have that characteristic smell, that funk, then the music, or what you are, is not valuable. The very tools the white man gave the Negro are suddenly used against him. These very weapons he has given us. (*AB*, p. 59)

Baraka's "the very tools the white man gave the Negro are suddenly used against him" strongly echoes Sartre's "a Black man who turns it against them and gives it a rigorously defined function." When Baraka refers to jazz as "American dada" he suggests that jazz incorporates the same violence and chaos as dada-surrealism and can be put to the same revisionary uses. In this way, Baraka fuses European dada and American black music. For instance, in "The Screamers," from *Tales* (1967), the character Lynn Hope uses his music to bring the black masses to dada riot. This story anticipates the disciplined violence of the later Marxist stage. In addition, in the same story Baraka refers to Jay McNeely, the hornplayer, as "the first Dada coon" and compares him to Marcel Duchamp: "On his back he [McNeely] screaming was the Mona Lisa with the mustache, as crude and simple" (*T*, p. 76–77). As in Duchamp's famous mock defacing of the Mona Lisa, in Baraka's story McNeely defaces high art in order to create something new and vital. In Baraka's view, both he and Duchamp are involved in creative destruction. But Duchamp's graffiti are finally not as complete as Baraka's: the French artist's work stays within the house of art, while Baraka's goes out into the street. Baraka wants to move from the "quiet music" of white poetry to the scream of black music and to the purifying violence of physical warfare. Unlike many of his black American predecessors, he does not want to be a refined black writer. Rather, he wants to be the direct revolutionary artist. At the time of "Screamers" he wanted to bring the black masses to dada riot; today he wants to bring the black proletariat to revolution. To turn himself into the poet who can call his people to action, Baraka employs the jazz aesthetic process to strip away his spurious white sophistication.

2. The Radical White Avant-garde

The post–World War II avant-garde—including the Beat Generation, the Black Mountain Poets, and the New York School—has a strong sense of continuity; these artists think of themselves as the continuation of the pre–World War I radical modernists.[1] In his introduction to *The Moderns* (1963), Baraka argues:

> The concerns that made [contemporary avant-garde] poetry seem so new were merely that the writers who were identified with this recent poetic renaissance were continuing the tradition of twentieth century modernism that had been initiated in the early part of this century. William Carlos Williams, Ezra Pound, The Imagists, and the French symbolist poets were restored to importance as beginners of a still vital tradition of Western poetry. It was an attempt to restore American poetry to the mainstream of modern poetry after it had been cut off from that tradition by the Anglo-Eliotic domination of the academies. (p. xi)

1. I have used the terms *post–World War II avant-garde, postmodernists,* and *contemporary avant-garde* interchangeably to refer to the three above-mentioned schools. Furthermore, the names of the above-mentioned schools are not intended as definitive terms but only as convenient and preexisting categories. For example, the term *New York School* might not be recognized by all critics, but the informed reader will know when I use the term that I am referring to a group of writers that certainly includes John Ashbery, Frank O'Hara, and James Schuyler, whether the group ever existed as group qua group. Moreover, Baraka was profoundly influenced by central members of all three groups—Charles Olson (Black Mountain Poets), Allen Ginsberg (the Beat Generation), and Frank O'Hara (The New York School). The terms *post–World War II avant-garde, postmodernists,* and *contemporary avant-garde* are not precise, but they are convenient if the reader understands their very limited meaning. There is nothing theoretical about them—they simply refer to experimental schools that appeared in America in the midforties. I realize that *postmodernist* is the woolliest of the three, but I have kept it because it is easy to distinguish from *modernist.* I want the reader to know at a glance whether I am discussing the pre–World War I avant-garde or the post–World World II avant-garde. *Radical modernists* refers to the pre–World War I aesthetically, but not necessarily politically, radical wing of modernism—in particular, Pound and Williams, who continued the revolutionary free-verse innovations initiated by Walt Whitman. *Radical avant-garde* applies to both the radical modernists and the postmodernists.

Octavio Paz rightly contends that the Anglo-American poetic modernist tradition is a restoring one[2]—one that resuscitates prior innovations and ideas—and Baraka and the postmodernists are faithful to this tenet by continuing the restoration in their generation. Both generations of the white avant-garde exercised a positive influence on Amiri Baraka's poetry and poetics. With the other members of the younger generation, Baraka inherited from the modernists the contention that the oral tradition is a principal source of poetry and the notion of verse as spoken, didactic, communicative, and political. From his avant-garde peers Baraka absorbed the Projectivists' poetic mode, the autobiographical approach, and the dada-surrealist method. Both white avant-garde traditions provided him with models that he adapted to fit his particular needs.

1.

It has become a commonplace to say that Amiri Baraka has been influenced by the Projectivist School; no one, however, has made it clear how profound and lasting this influence has been. The main source of influence is the great white whale of American literature, Charles Olson. Olson was the "source of fire" not only for Baraka but also for an entire post–World War II generation of young American poets, including Robert Creeley, Robert Duncan, Denise Levertov, Edward Dorn, and others. First from Black Mountain College in North Carolina, then later from Gloucester, Massachusetts, Olson provided the poetics for the younger avant-garde poets. At the time, Gilbert Sorrentino asserted: "Olson is our Ezra Pound" (*SA*, p. 49). From the Projectivists, and from Olson in particular, Baraka absorbed his sense of the poem as open form, his sense of line, his sense of the poem as a recorder of process, and his conception of the poem as definition and exploration. For instance, speaking of form, Baraka has said: "There must not be any preconceived notion or design for what a poem ought to be. 'Who knows what a poem ought to sound like? Until it's thar' says Charles Olson . . . & I follow closely with that. I'm not interested in writing sonnets, sestina or anything . . . only poems" (*N*, p. 425).

2. *Children of the Mire: Modern Poetry from Romanticism to the Avant-Garde,* p. 123.

The Projectivists taught Baraka to think of a poem as a way to understand and reveal the world. Denise Levertov maintains, "For me, back of the idea of organic form is the concept that there is a form in all things (and in our experience) which the poet can discover and reveal."[3] Further, as Robert Creeley states, "The process of definition is the intent of the poem" (*N*, p. 408), and Levertov echoes: "A partial definition, then, of organic poetry might be that it is a method of apperception, i.e., of recognizing what we perceive. . . . Such poetry is exploratory."[4] The Projectivist tradition is an Objectivist-Imagist one, and the Objectivist tradition from Pound to Olson has believed that the poet brings information about the world into his poems. In his role as a Projectivist, Baraka asserts: "Poetry is not a form, but rather a result. Whatever the matter, its meaning, if precise enough in its information (and direction) of the world, is poetic. . . . I write poetry only to enlist the poetic consistently as apt description of my life. I write poetry only in order to feel, and that, finally, sensually, all the terms of my life. I write poetry to investigate myself, and my meaning and meanings. . . . But also to invest the world with a clearer understanding of it self, but only by virtue of my having brought some clearer understanding to my self into it" (*BMP*, p. 41).

Charles Olson almost single-handedly made the line the main rhythmic unit of postmodernist poetry. Whether or not what Olson said about the breath unit is true—"the line comes (I swear it) from the breath, from the breathing of the man who writes, at the moment that he writes" (*SW*, p. 19)—the poem has been mercilessly chopped by Projectivists into breath units.[5] Although Baraka followed Olson's lead, he was quite conscious of his own modifications; as he explains:

3. *The Poet in the World* (New York: New Directions, 1973), p. 7.

4. Ibid.

5. Unexpectedly, Karl Shapiro and Robert Beum lend support to Olson's controversial theory of the breath unit: "Keeping in mind that poetry is essentially an oral art intended for recitation in some form, and not for the printed page (despite modern leaning toward the 'silent' poem), we can observe something about the line in terms of breathing. We quite naturally desire units of verse that will not leave us breathless. At rest, we draw a breath about every four seconds. An English iambic pentameter line usually consumes no less than two and no more than four seconds." *A Prosody Handbook* (New York: Harper & Row, 1965), p. 46.

I don't mean that I write poems completely the way I'm talking now, although I'm certain that a great deal of my natural voice rhythm dominates the lines. For instance, my breathing—when I have to stop to inhale or exhale—dictates where I have to break the line in most cases. Sometimes I can bring the line out longer to effect—you learn certain tricks, departures from a set method. But mostly it's the rhythms of speech that I utilize, trying to get closer to the way I sound peculiarly, as opposed to somebody else. (*SA*, p. 80)

Baraka also acquired the idea of the poetics of flux from Olson. In *The Special View of History* (given as lectures in 1956, published in 1970) Olson states, "PROCESS—what Heraclitus tried on as 'flux'—is reality,"[6] and the poet's job is to write about the flux. Robert von Hallberg says of Olson, "He felt that this poetry must engage the flux of reality. He believed—and found confirmation of this belief in Heraclitus and Whitehead—that reality is an unceasing process which undermines all static achievements. Hence, all preconceived forms, in fact, all closure, is unfaithful to reality. Olson engaged this matter in moral terms: in order to fulfill its moral obligation, art must commit itself—no matter the painful uncertainty—to process, to open form."[7] Not only Projectivist Olson but also Objectivist Williams before him had wanted to "seize the moment."[8] Baraka is also fully committed to seizing the moment. In fact, even the title of his 1964 essay on poetics indicates what tradition he is in: "Hunting Is Not Those Heads on the Wall" (*H*, p. 176). That is, the art process, the exploration, is more important than the art object.

"Seizing the moment" is an active process, and Baraka learned the value of the verb from Olson. It follows that Olson's poetry, poetry of the flux, would also be a poetry that emphasizes the verb. In "Projective Verse" (an essay Baraka thought highly of and published in his Totem Press series), Olson complains about Hart Crane's overuse of the noun and sings the merits of the verb: "But there is a loss in Crane of what Fenollosa is so right about, in syntax, the sentence as first act of nature, as

6. Charles Olson, *The Special View of History*, ed. Ann Charters, p. 42.
7. *Charles Olson: The Scholar's Art*, p. 72.
8. William Carlos Williams, *Paterson*, p. 35.

lightning, as passage of force from subject to object, quick, in this case, from Hart to me, in every case, from me to you, the VERB, between two nouns" (*SW*, p. 21). Baraka extends Olson's idea: "The academic Western mind is the best example of the substitution of artifact worship for the lightning awareness of the art process. Even the artist is more valuable than his artifact, because the art process goes on in his mind. But the process itself is the most important quality because it can transform and create, and its only form is possibility" (*H*, p. 174). Because Baraka thinks of the art process as a verb process, he describes it as "lightning awareness," which echoes Olson's depiction of the verb as "lightning." In *Home*, Baraka developed Olson's ideas about form and verb power:

> Formal art, that is, artifacts made to cohere to preconceived forms, is almost devoid of this verb value. Usually a man playing Bach is only demonstrating his music lessons; the contemporary sonneteer, his ability to organize intellectual materials. But nothing that already exists is that valuable. The most valuable quality in life is the will to existence, the unconnected zoom, which finally becomes in anyone's hand whatever part of it he could collect. Like dipping cups of water from the falls. Which is what the artist does. Fools want to dictate what kind of dipper he uses. (p. 175)

Olson helped Baraka shape his poems, provided him with his concept of surging reality, but, interestingly, the metaphor for reality, the falls, comes from William Carlos Williams.

2.

The postmodernists, feeling that the years after World War II were impersonal, repressed, and conformist, created a highly individualistic autobiographic poetry to counter the times. Such avant-gardists as Frank O'Hara and Allen Ginsberg, in their very different styles, wanted to put "real people," including themselves, into their poems and to detail them in all their charming oddness. They saw self-expression and even exhibitionism as techniques to liberate both the poet and his society from the restraints of the era. Amiri Baraka felt the same urge to rebel against conformity and anonymity, and from the rebels he learned to use the autobiographical mode as a weapon against the age.

"Nakedness," says John Tytell, "signified rebirth, the recovery of identity" for the post modernists.[9] Ginsberg asked America "when will you be angelic? / When will you take off your clothes?"[10] For the contemporary avant-garde, especially the Beat Generation, good poetry begins with self-revelation— "good craft" is measured by the degree to which the poet gets the real self in the poem; "it's the ability to write the same way that you are," said Allen Ginsberg in his famous 1965 *Paris Review* interview. This interview made a central and engaging statement about autobiographical candor and the new literature that explains some of the detailed presence of these poets in their own work. For Ginsberg, "literature is identical with sincerity"; speaking for himself, Ginsberg comments:

> The problem is, where it gets to literature, is this, we all talk among ourselves and we have common understanding, and we say anything we want to say, and we talk about our ass-holes, and we talk about our cocks, and we talk about who we fucked last night, or who we're gonna fuck tomorrow, or what kind of love affair we have, or when we got drunk, or when we stuck a broom in our ass in the Hotel Ambassador in Prague—anybody tells one's friends about that. So then—what happens if you make a distinction between what you tell your friends and what you tell your Muse? The problem is to break down that distinction: when you approach the Muse to talk as frankly as you would talk with yourself or with your friends. So I began finding, in conversations with Burroughs and Kerouac and Gregory Corso, in conversations with people whom I respected, that things we were telling each other for real were totally different from what was already in literature. And that was Kerouac's great discovery in *On the Road*. The kinds of things that he and Neal Cassady were talking about, he finally discovered were *the* subject matter for what he wanted to write down. That meant, at that minute, a complete revision of what literature was supposed to be, in his mind, and actually in the minds of the people

9. *Naked Angels: The Lives and Literature of the Beat Generation*, p. 4.
10. *Howl and Other Poems*, p. 31.

that first read the book. . . . It's the ability to write, the same
way that you are!"[11]

Here, Ginsberg claims that the poet's entire life should be pre-
sented in his poems—that nothing should be kept from the
Muse, including the autobiographical self. I have quoted Gins-
berg in such detail both because this passage embodies the stan-
dards of autobiographical candor (whatever you tell your friends
you tell the Muse) and because it is an example itself of the
uninhibited autobiographical art that influenced Baraka. In fact,
this passage shows how perfect a genre the interview is for
spontaneous, self-confessing artists. Like the diary, it imposes
no false structures (such as plot and character) between the
writer and his audience. In addition, this interview shows that
the idea of the autobiographical, at least in the Beat world, grew
out of conversations within that community rather than out of
some abstract program; as they discussed their lives and their
art, the Beats discovered that their personal adventures were
suitable subject matter for their art. Having objectives similar to
Ginsberg's, Baraka declared, "I make a poetry with what I feel
is useful & can be saved out of all the garbage of our lives. What
I see, am touched by (CAN HEAR) . . . wives, gardens, jobs,
cement yards where cats pee, all my interminable artifacts . . .
ALL are a poetry & nothing moves (with any grace) pried apart
from these things" (*N*, p. 424).

Because Baraka is a part of this autobiographical tradition, the
"I" in his poems is a fairly close approximation to himself. Re-
jecting the persona, he substitutes an autobiographical speaker:
"Let my poems be a graph / of me" he proclaims in "Balboa, The
Entertainer" (*DL*, p. 10). Identification of the narrator of most of
Baraka's poems with the author is, then, appropriate. With oth-
ers of his generation, he was consciously involved in overthrow-
ing the mask theory of poetry—the impersonal theory of Eliot
and the New Criticism that the "I" of the poem is a fictive verbal
being unrelated to the person who created it. As Walter Sutton
has summarized the Eliotic theory of poetry; "The poem is not
self-expression, the direct statement of the personal emotions of

---

11. Thomas Clark, "Allen Ginsberg," in *Writers at Work: The Paris Review
Interviews,* Third Series, ed. George Plimpton, pp. 287–88. The opening quo-
tation about sincerity is by Alfred Kazin and comes from his "Introduction"
to the collection (p. x).

the author; it is rather an impersonal formulation of common feelings and emotions which need not be experienced at first hand."[12] But, while the mask theory of poetry applies very well to certain kinds of poetry—especially poems in the Eliotic tradition—it does not apply to poetry with such lines as:

> I'm Everett LeRoi Jones, 30 yrs old.
> A black nigger in the universe. A long breath singer,
> would be dancer
> . . . .
> I am a meditative man. And when I say something it's
> all of me
> saying, and all the things that make me, have formed me,
> colored me
> this brilliant night. (*BMP*, pp. 47–48)

The late Kenneth Rexroth, bohemia's elder statesman, observed of the new avant-garde: "No avant garde American poet accepts the I. A. Richards-Valery thesis that a poem is an end in itself, an anonymous machine for providing aesthetic experience. All believe in poetry as communication, statement from one person to another" (*C*, p. 191). And Jack Kerouac, who wanted to use real names in *On the Road* but was dissuaded by his publisher, Viking,[13] declared, "The best writing is always the most painfully personal wrung-out tossed from cradle warm protective mind—tap from yourself the song of yourself, blow!—now!—your way is your only way—'Good' or 'bad'—always honest, ('ludicrous'), spontaneous, 'confessional' interesting, because not 'crafted.' Craft is craft" (*C*, p. 66).

Because Baraka is so committed to the autobiographical mode, to use the standard New Critical device of referring to the "I" of a Baraka poem as a persona is to miss its spirit if not its meaning. Even sensitive readers like Houston Baker and Kimberly Benston fall back on such New Critical terms as *speaker* and *poet*.[14] Although such "impersonal" readings do not necessarily

12. *American Free Verse*, p. 37.

13. *Naked Angels*, p. 157.

14. See Houston A. Baker's " 'These Are Songs if You Have the / Music': An Essay on Imamu Baraka," pp. 1–18; Kimberly W. Benston's *Baraka: The Renegade and the Mask;* and Lloyd W. Brown's *Amiri Baraka*. In *Amiri Baraka/ LeRoi Jones*, Werner Sollors is sensitive to the autobiographical nature of Baraka's art.

generate poor interpretations, they do sidestep the issue of the person in the poem, a central question of the contemporary avant-garde; they also allow critics to ignore their own aesthetic standards of sincerity, a topic to be returned to in my discussion of Ginsberg. Critic Lloyd Brown illustrates the dangers of bringing the wrong standards to bear. Brown, who has written a book on Jane Austen, seeks irony and control in Baraka—standards appropriate for Austen but inappropriate for an artist like Baraka who does not overvalue irony and control but seeks an art of incitement and destruction. To say that a poet attempts to portray himself in a poem does not mean the reader must take him at his word, but it does mean that the reader must approach the poem with different expectations and even standards than one would use in approaching poems imitating the "well-wrought urn" tradition.

For instance, "For Hettie," a poem about Baraka's first wife, Hettie Cohen, is not a poem divorced from his everyday life, a poem that in some way stylizes a biographical woman; rather, it grows out of the domestic life of a married bohemian in the late 1950s:

> My wife is left-handed
> which implies a fierce de-
> termination. ITS WEIRD, BABY.
> The way some folks
> are always trying to be
> different. A sin & a shame.   (*P*, p. 13)

This lighthearted poem also illustrates Baraka's poetic contention that a poem can—and should—incorporate any subject, no matter how mundane. In Baraka's autobiographical mode, the only principle of selection is that the subject come from his life.

In a more sober mood—in his cultural nationalist phase—Baraka explored his personal past. In "Leroy," he meditates on a photograph of his mother:

> I wanted to know my mother when she sat
> looking sad across campus in the late 20's
> into the future of the soul, there were black angels
> straining above her head, carrying life from our ancestors
> and knowledge, and the strong nigger feeling.   (*BMP*, p. 217)

Here, the mother passes on the wisdom of the black tradition to her son, as it was passed on to her. In these poems the autobiographical element is important because it places the subject in time and within family relationships. In the closing lines Baraka wills his own inheritance, his "sweet" black legacy, to his people:

> When I die, the consciousness I carry I will to
> black people. May they pick me apart and take the
> useful parts, the sweet meat of my feelings. And leave
> the bitter bullshit rotten white parts
> alone   (*BMP*, p. 217)

Like Ginsberg, Baraka feels that his whole self must be in his poem ("when I say something it's all of me / saying, and all the things that make me, have formed me, colored me") and summons readers to a presence of love that springs from a temporal recognition of the self: "today is the history we must learn to desire. . . . There is no guilt in love" (*BMP*, p. 48).

In addition to Allen Ginsberg, Frank O'Hara of the New York School also gave Baraka ideas about the autobiographical poem. Baraka mused about his indebtedness: "O'Hara's openness and Ginsberg's openness might have influenced me because finally I wanted to write in a way that was direct and in that I could say the things I wanted to say, even about myself, and maybe that did help me to lose any restraints" ("HI," pp. 21–22). Frank O'Hara's poems celebrate the personal, including one LeRoi Jones who "walks into" an O'Hara poem, appropriately entitled "Personal Poem":

> And LeRoi comes in
> and tells me Miles Davis was clubbed 12
> times last night outside BIRDLAND by a cop.[15]

In 1960 Baraka defended the autobiographical elements in the O'Hara poem, which, incidentally, he published in his magazine, *Yugen*.

> I didn't especially think that there was any charted-out area in which the poetic sensibility had to function to make a poem.

15. *The Selected Poems*, p. 157.

> . . . Anybody who is concerned with the poem will get it on an emotional level. . . . I don't see what makes it any less valid because it's a casual kind of reference or that it comes out of a person's life, rather than, say, from his academic life. (*SA*, p. 79)

Of his own first experiment in personal poetry in 1959, O'Hara reminisced:

> When I was writing it [the poem] I was realizing that if I wanted to I could use the telephone instead of writing the poem, and so Personism was born. It's a very exciting movement. . . . It puts the poem squarely between the poet and the person. . . . The poem is at last between two persons instead of two pages. (*PN*, pp. 354, 355)

Even though O'Hara's statement is in part self-mocking, it speaks for the postwar avant-garde's new sense of the need for the personal and the interpersonal in art; poetry becomes an act of communication between two persons, not personae. Ginsberg expresses it as "the ability to write, the same way that you are!," and O'Hara declares, "It puts the poem squarely between the poet and the person." These two statements express the essence of the autobiographical poem. From "Lately, I've become accustomed to the way / The ground opens up and envelopes me" from Baraka's first book, *Preface* (1961, p. 5), to "I'd / call you Amina, Afrikan faith" from *Hard Facts* (1975, p. 3), to "If Don Lee thinks I am imitating him in this poem, / this is only payback for his imitating me" from *Poetry for the Advanced* (1979, *SP*, p. 336), the "I" of the poem is LeRoi Jones/Amiri Baraka speaking.

3.

One of the signs of the American avant-garde's distrust of Western rationalism was its resurrection of the European dadaist and surrealist movements during the post–World War II period. The Beat Generation, especially Allen Ginsberg and Gregory Corso, borrowed from dada to achieve its aims; the New York School, in particular Frank O'Hara and John Ashbery,[16] borrowed from surrealism. Ginsberg and Corso used

---

16. Dada and surrealism influenced both the postmodernist and other contemporary schools of poetry. See Paul Zweig's helpful essay, "The New Surrealism," pp. 269–84. For useful introductions to dada and surrealism, see

dada glee to disrupt the respectable middle-class world by shocking its genteel sensibilities; O'Hara and Ashbery used surrealist imagery to catapult readers into amazing surreal worlds. Collectively these poets led American poetry away from mundane realism and into the world of dreams and the fantastic. They followed André Breton, the great surrealist theoretician, when he declared: "I believe in the future resolution of these two states, dream and reality, which are seemingly so contradictory, into a kind of absolute reality, a surreality, if one may so speak."[17] They also reflect Breton's valuation of "the Marvelous" as the only authentic standard for the beautiful: "Let us not mince words; the marvelous is always beautiful, anything marvelous is beautiful, in fact only the marvelous is beautiful." For these postmodernists, the marvelous is a glimpsing of a higher reality, beyond the contradictions of dream and reality, conscious and unconscious.

Surrealism and dada were important to the members of the post–World War II avant-garde because they wanted to shock, to astonish, and thereby to break down traditional ideas of reality. They were drawn to dada and surrealism for the same reasons they were drawn to Zen Buddhism and existentialism: they found the Western tradition spiritually and emotionally incomplete. As Western artists, they began to question the vitality and utility of their tradition. William Barrett asserts: "That Western painters and sculptors have in this century gone outside their own tradition to nourish themselves on the art of the rest of the world—Oriental, African, Melanesian—signifies that what we have known as *the* tradition is no longer able to nourish its most creative members: the confining mold of this tradition has broken, under pressures both from within and without."[18] Finding

---

C. W. E. Bigsby's *Dada and Surrealism* and Mary Ann Caws's *The Poetry of Dada and Surrealism: Aragon, Breton, Tzara, Eluard, and Desnos.* Even though I do make distinctions between dada and surrealism, I do not want to put too fine a point on it. Individual postmodernists were influenced by both schools, and only sometimes is it useful to make distinctions between them. Furthermore, it is hard to draw a definite line between the two schools. Caws summarizes the sentiments of Michel Sanouillet, the dadaist, in the following way: "[He] calls surrealism 'the French form of Dada,' and maintains that Dada and surrealism are altering waves of the same spirit" (p. 7).

17. This and subsequent quotations are from André Breton's *Manifestoes of Surrealism*, p. 14.

18. *Irrational Man*, p. 47.

their own tradition too abstract and cut off from the nourishment of God and nature, these artists have reached out to other traditions to reestablish what Nietzsche terms contact with the earth. They are seeking a poetry of immanence and presence, a poetry of the here and now, in contrast to what they see as a poetry of the past; in this quest, of course, they are part of a movement that began with the Victorians and the early modernists. In fact, one theme of modernity is the fragmentation and insufficiency of the Western tradition to sustain itself, a theme that has led poets touched with nihilism to describe the tradition as a mere "heap of broken images." Irving Howe catalogs the modernist's disasters:

> The modernist sensibility posits a blockage, if not an end, to history: an apocalyptic *cul de sac* in which both teleological ends and secular process are called into question, perhaps become obsolete. Man is mired—you can take your choice—in the mass, in the machine, in the city, in his loss of faith, in the hopelessness of a life without anterior intention or terminal value. By this late time, these disasters seem in our imaginations to have merged into one.[19]

Dada and surrealism were two ways in which European artists, and then the American avant-garde, sought to awaken their audiences to recognition of the Western crisis. Even more than his contemporaries, Baraka had reason to absorb and transform dadaist and surrealist techniques. In the dada mode discussed in Chapter 1, Baraka transforms random dada violence into disciplined political violence to be used to attack Western culture; he radicalizes the dada Ginsberg had employed as an *enfant terrible*. The other method, the focus of this section, is the surrealistic mode. This, too, Baraka bends to his own peculiar needs.

It is important to note that, with the exception of Philip Lamantia, none of the American postmodernists was a doctrinaire disciple of surrealism and André Breton. For them, Breton was a guide to new possibilities, not a dictator of aesthetic principles. Rather than doctrine, these writers embraced surrealist techniques, and they did not all embrace them to the same de-

---

19. "Introduction: The Idea of the Modern," in *Literary Modernism*, ed. Irving Howe (New York: A Fawcett Premier Book, 1967), p. 15.

gree. Ginsberg embraced a language of free association that liberated his poems from linear progression: Corso, O'Hara, and Ashbery forged worlds out of the irrational. Moreover, few of the poets dogmatically employed automatic writing to gain the marvelous, a central device of surrealism.

Baraka, like his contemporaries, took on surrealist techniques without surrealist dogma. Baraka uses surrealism in four ways: first, he uses dream/fantasy imagery to exaggerate reality, creating moral allegories; second, he employs the bizarre conceit, the odd coupling of surreal imagery, for the pure pleasure of the bizarreness; third, he uses surrealist imagery to legitimate his own flights into fantasy; and, finally, he uses surrealist imagery to reflect his own psychic state. Baraka does embrace the "dereglement de tous les sens," but not, as did the surrealists, to achieve a higher reality; rather, he values it for the odd effects it produces, effects that, for him, highlight the real world. Although he sometimes also enjoys flights of the imagination for their own sake, Baraka's flights grow out of the fantasy world of his childhood; surrealism simply legitimates his own imaginative worlds.

John Ashbery, in such poems as "The Instruction Manual" and "Mixed Feelings"—in which he wants to escape the mundane world into a fantastic one—exhibits a similar use of surrealism as a legitimation for his own imaginative flights. In "Mixed Feelings" Ashbery projects himself into a 1942 photograph of "girls lounging around / An old fighter bomber" and so values his escape that he claims not to mind the domination of his created "creatures" over his own self: "I am not offended that these creatures (that's the word) / Of my imagination seem to hold me in such light esteem."[20] Like Baraka, Ashbery uses images from American popular culture and free associationist techniques from surrealism in poems such as "Farm Implements and Rutabagas in a Landscape." Unlike Ashbery, however, Baraka has spent his career trying to escape the "creatures . . . of my imagination"; for him, fantasy, while compelling, is an escape from the sociopolitical reality he must bring himself to face. Yet Baraka's struggle against the attractions of surrealist fantasies is also expressed in surrealist terms: "I am inside

20. John Ashbery, *A Geography of Poets*, ed. Edward Field (New York: Bantam Books, 1979), p. 435.

someone / who hates me," he laments in "An Agony. As Now" (*DL*, p. 15).

Baraka's surrealism is not the "pure" surrealism of the young Frank O'Hara in such poems as those in *Second Avenue* (written in 1953, published in 1960 by Baraka's Totem Press), poems of radical incoherence, or of Gregory Corso in such poems as "The Mad Yak," from *Gasoline* (1958), poems of zany irrationality. In general, Baraka uses surrealism as a way to magnify reality. He commented on surrealism in 1980:

> I have always valued . . . that as one approach to art . . . to actually create worlds in which strange things happen, but these strange things really relate to the real world. Strange or bizarre or seemingly impossible happenings are simply exaggerated realities. . . . [I am r]eally trying to exaggerate reality in such a way that people can understand it better. In a recent play of mine, "The Relationship of the Lone Ranger to the Means of Production," having the Lone Ranger be Uncle Sam with a mask on you know, what I mean—walking around the factory—is really exaggerating reality, making a bizarre circumstance so as to make a point in real life. ("HI," pp. 22–23)

Magnifying reality is, for the didactic Baraka (espcially in his Marxist stage), a way to create sociopolitical allegories, to extend and exaggerate ordinary circumstances in order to shock the reader into a reevaluation of his own dilemma. In "The Relationship of the Lone Ranger to the Means of Production" he draws on images from popular culture to intensify the effect:

Donna:	Who are you, mister?
Masked Man:	You can call me MM.
Reg:	MM . . . what's that stand for?
Masked Man:	It could be Masked Man . . .
Clark:	This guy is from management, in that get up. He's an owner. MM stands for masked man, alright.
Masked Man:	It could be, but my friends call me mmmmm, for sweet.
Reg:	Who are you, mister, you must be with management otherwise they'd toss you out. No visitors or strangers on the plant floor.
Masked Man:	My real name is Money's Master.

Donna: Of course, and Masked Man, too, and mmmm
            because we are in the united snakes and bour-
            geois ideology dressed up sweetlike.

(SP, pp. 255–56)

Here, as elsewhere, Baraka's goal, like the surrealists', is "to
create a new kind of vision, not to transcribe a vision already
glimpsed."[21] Unlike the surrealists, in "The Lone Ranger" Bar-
aka's "vision" is didactic. Once again, he has inverted a popular
image to suit his own needs: for the young Baraka, as for most
Americans, the Lone Ranger represented moral justice. Baraka
took the values of his childhood, values that sprang from pop-
ular culture, seriously: "They [popular heroes] taught us that
evil needed to be destroyed" (*A*, p. 21). Today, however, Baraka
has inverted that image, making the Lone Ranger represent the
capitalist, bourgeois individualism, the ethos of a ruthless soci-
ety. Today he seeks collective, not individual, solutions to social
problems, and the object of presenting the Lone Ranger as a
capitalist is to illustrate Baraka's contention that our cultural
heroes are actually bandits exploiting the masses. Moreover,
inverting the icon of the Lone Ranger (from lawman to interna-
tional outlaw) casts doubt on every aspect of bourgeois idealism
and provides a way for Baraka to exorcise that idealism from
himself. By making his culture heroes "masked" exploiters, he
is turning a loved image into a hated one in order to reject it:
"Marx, Donald Duck, Einstein, are all the same source. You can
learn from them" (*R*, p. 104), he declared in his cultural nation-
alist stage.

But Baraka also uses surrealist images for pure poetic delight,
which accounts for some of the obscurity of his poetry, espe-
cially in the early work. In *Tales* (1967) we find this surreal con-
ceit: "I am a poet. I am a rich famous butcher. I am the man
who paints the gold balls on the tops of flagpoles. I am, no
matter, more beautiful than anyone else" (*T*, p. 29). Not unlike
John Ashbery in his "The Instruction Manual," he takes
the reader on a flight of the imagination. The persona in the
Ashbery poem escapes his dreary job of writing instruction
manuals by dreaming of being transported to a fantasized
Guadalajara. Ashbery confides:

21. Caws, *Poetry of Dada*, p. 20.

> And, as my way is, I begin to dream, resting my elbows on the
>   desk and leaning out of the window a little,
> Of dim Guadalajara! City of rose-colored flowers!   (*N*, p. 272)

Similarly, Baraka juxtaposes bizarre and apparently unrelated
images to take the reader beyond the rational world into a world
where the artist's beauty is embodied in his uselessness, in his
total impracticality. Someone asks the poet, "What do you do
for a living?" "Oh, me," replies the poet, "nothing special; I
paint gold balls on the top of flagpoles." Delighting in the bi-
zarre, Baraka plunges the reader into that apparently aimless
world.

Like other contemporary avant-gardists, Baraka often
achieved his surreal flight with the assistance of the pop imagi-
nation. In "In Memory of Radio," written in the late 1950s, Bar-
aka states:

> Saturday mornings we listened to *Red Lantern* & his
>   undersea folk.
> At 11, *Let's Pretend*/& we did/& I, the poet, still do,
>   Thank God!   (*P*, p. 12)

At that time the poet pretended, lived in the imagination; with
Ashbery and O'Hara, he found popular culture the avenue to
the imagination. The American child's escape from adult reali-
ties is also, it seems, a deeply embedded avenue to fantasy for
many adults. Ashbery, for instance, uses popular imagery in
such poems as "Farm Implements and Rutabagas," where he
escapes not to a fancied Guadalajara but to the house of Popeye,
into a world where the Popeye story is retold in Wagnerian
tones. Similarly, in "To a Publisher" Baraka takes a flight on the
pop imagination:

> I long to be a mountain climber
> & wave my hands up 8,000 feet.
> Out of sight & snow blind/the tattered
> Stars and Stripes poked in the new peak.
>
> & come down later, Clipper[22] by my side,
> To new wealth & eternal fame. That
> kind of care. I could wear
> Green corduroy coats & felt tyroleans
> For the rest of my days; & belong to clubs.   (*P*, p. 19)

22. The canine companion of the forties radio hero, Sky King.

This enthusiasm for pop is not limited to the New York School. The Beats also celebrated that mad world. In "In Memory of Radio" Baraka begins with this question:

> Who had ever stopped to think of the divinity of
>   Lamont Cranston?
> (Only Jack Kerouac, that I know of: & Me.)   (*P*, p. 12)

In fact, in "The Origins of the Beat Generation," Kerouac rhapsodically lists the sources of the Beat spirit: "the completely senseless babble of the Three Stooges, the ravings of the Marx Brothers, . . . Krazy Kat with the irrational brick, . . . the frantic Shadow going mwee hee heee ha ha in the alleys of New York imagination" (*C*, p. 71). The pop world attracted Kerouac because it expressed a mad anarchy: it is a spiritual source of American dada and surrealism. Certainly one reason Baraka was drawn to the bohemians was their shared enthusiasm for this childhood legacy. As a child, Kerouac had sat enraptured before the radio in Lowell, Massachusetts; similarly, Baraka sat enraptured in Newark, New Jersey. For both—as for many Americans—popular culture was a source of the Marvelous. The bohemians were important to Baraka in part because they not only respected pop subject matter but also provided examples of how to incorporate it into high art. Baraka, commenting on one source of his surrealism, science fiction, shows the connection between the two: "There were definitely some surreal elements in some of those things, surreal or fantasy. My early reading was science fiction. So I have never felt constrained by quote 'surface' realism" ("HI," p. 23).

Finally, surreal techniques help Baraka express states of mind he could not express with any other method. In *Tales* he declares, "To stand at the end of feeling because I couldn't use it" (p. 111), suggesting both concretely and precisely a psychic state in which the protagonist no longer wants an emotion he does not find useful. As we have already noted, in "An Agony. As Now" (1964) he cries, "I am inside someone / who hates me," and continues,

>   . . . I look
> out from his eyes. Smell
> what fouled tunes come in
> to his breath   (*DL*, p. 15)

Poems like these show the schizophrenic state of being a black man in a white world who feels a growing allegiance elsewhere; they describe a man divided against himself. In fact, these lines suggest similar ones from Frank O'Hara's radically surreal poem "In Memory of Feeling":

> My quietness had a man in it, he is transparent
> and carries me quietly, like a gondola, through the streets.
> He has several likenesses,
>   like stars and years, like numerals.   (*N*, p. 244)

Both poems involve a split consciousness. In his poem Baraka describes the conflict he feels being a black man living in a corrupt white world. In his, O'Hara delineates the conflict between the ordinary self and the artistic self. Marjorie Perloff argues, "The poet's old self must die if it is to be reborn"[23]—reborn as an artistic self. For Baraka, the split in self could only be healed by rejecting his old white self for a new black one. In his bohemian days, Baraka's Beat self was always "publicly redefining each change in my self" (*DL*, p. 79) because he was unsure of his identity. After he had created a new identity for himself, when he had found his place in the black world, he could declare:

> We are strange in a way because we know
> who we are. Black beings passing through
> a tortured passage of flesh.   (*BMP*, p. 177)

Baraka has continued to use surrealist methods throughout his career. During his black nationalist stage (1965–1974) his surrealist sensibility was at work creating such conceits as "Blue whitie" to refer to white people and "strumming my head / for a living" (*BMP*, p. 38) to refer to writing. In his Marxist stage (1974 to the present) he uses the figure of the Lone Ranger—no longer a childhood hero, but an adult villain—to attack imperialism. He is, in fact, an amazingly consistent poet for someone who is always being called mercurial. In the context of his entire career, it is clear that surrealism provided Baraka with techniques to express the particulars of his ever-changing situation.

23. *Frank O'Hara: Poet Among Painters,* p. 143.

4.

From Eliot to Ginsberg, fighters in this century's revolution of the word have had as one of their points of focus the problem of recapturing the sound of speech on the written page. To counter the silencing effect of the printing press, the avant-garde poet, whether modernist or contemporary avant-gardist, tried to place the human voice in his poems. The modernists focused primarily on orality as common speech; the contemporary avant-gardists concerned themselves with a fuller range, incorporating into their poems reverberations of jazz, the nasal tones of the street singer, and the hypnotic rhythms of the chant, as well as the human voice. They wanted both to democratize the poem and to expand its aural possibilities.

This emphasis on orality has made the white avant-garde an important influence on twentieth-century black literature. Before the 1920s, most black poetry had been stilted and conventional; it unimaginatively copied nineteenth-century British forms in order to legitimate itself in white eyes. The white avant-garde, with its new forms and ideas, acted as a catalyst to liberate black literature from antiquated ideas and forms. Ironically, these white writers helped the black writers, from Toomer to Baraka, fully to explore their own oral tradition, that linguistic complex that includes the folktale, oral history, black verbal style, the lyrics and even the musical settings of black songs. In this section I explore the white avant-garde's gift of orality to Baraka.

In the 1920s, with the poetry of Langston Hughes and Countee Cullen, the problem of black orality is clearly posed. On the one hand, Cullen's antique form contradicted his twentieth-century black experience. The language of such lines as the following does not jibe with the sounds of 1920s Harlem:

> My love is dark as yours is fair,
> Yet lovelier I hold her
> Than listless maids with pallid hair
> And blood that's thin and colder.[24]

While poets such as Cullen and Claude McKay denied black orality by writing poems that excluded black American sounds,

24. *Color*, p. 4.

Hughes, who wrote free verse and was well acquainted with modernism, could accommodate the blues and the black oral tradition into his poetry. In almost any poem of Hughes's we can see the smooth coupling of Afro-American expressive culture and poetic form. For example, in "Song for a Bango Dance," first published in 1922, we can hear the impact of everyday black speech and the blues form on Hughes's poetry:

> Shake your brown feet, honey,
> Shake your brown feet, chile
> Shake your brown feet, honey,
> Shake 'em swif and wil'
> > Get way back, honey
> > Do that low-down step.
> > Walk on over, darling,
> > > Now! Come out
> > > With your left.[25]

Hughes found that the free-verse blues was one appropriate form to embody the experience of black people. The most artistically successful poets of the Harlem Renaissance wrote in free verse: Hughes, Toomer, Sterling Brown. From Hughes and Toomer during the Harlem Renaissance, to Ellison during the 1940s and 1950s, to Baraka now, the flexibility of both form and conception has made avant-garde examples crucial and congenial for the black literary tradition.

Much of the white avant-garde shared an interest in the oral tradition. Olson refers to the pre–World War I radical modernists as "The Revolution of the ear, 1910" (*SW*, p. 15); Baraka refers to the post–World War II avant-garde as centrally concerned with "HOW YOU SOUND??" (*N*, p. 424). The new poetry from Pound and Williams through to the new generation is focused on speech rhythms. Interestingly, T. S. Eliot, the grand enemy of the radical avant-garde, shared similar ideas about the

---

25. Langston Hughes, *The Weary Blues*, p. 36. "Bango Dance" is only suggestive of the blues structure; in other poems, such as "Po' Boy Blues" (When I was home de / Sunshine seemed like gold. / When I was home de / sunshine seemed like gold. / Since I come up North de / Whole damn world's turned cold"), Hughes conforms totally to the rhyme pattern of this difficult form. For a good discussion of Hughes as a "blues poet," see James A. Emanuel's *Langston Hughes* (New Haven: College & University Press, 1967), pp. 137–43. "Po' Boy Blues" quoted from Emanuel.

importance of speech for the shaping of poetry. In "The Music of Poetry" (1957), Eliot declares:

> Every revolution in poetry is apt to be, and sometimes to announce itself to be, a return to common speech. That is the revolution which Wordsworth announced in his prefaces, and he was right; but the same revolution had been carried out a century before by Oldham, Waller, Denham and Dryden; and the same revolution was due again something over a century later. The followers of a revolution develop the new poetic idiom in one direction or another; they polish or perfect it; meanwhile the spoken language goes on changing, and the poetic idiom goes out of date. Perhaps we do not realize how natural the speech of Dryden must have sounded to the most sensitive of his contemporaries.[26]

Eliot not only believed in the importance of speech in any revolution of the word, which joins him conceptually with his more radical contemporaries, but he also offered one of the most compelling arguments for the revolution of the word. Like Eliot, Pound also felt that part of the modern poet's mission was to celebrate "the language of the tribe," to record the common speech of the people. In fact, perhaps one reason Pound and Eliot (and Baraka too) look back to Dante is that he wrote in the language of his people, in Italian instead of Latin; he made poetry out of the vernacular. Eliot says, "The language of Dante is the perfection of a common language."[27]

Continuing the vernacular tradition of Eliot, Pound, and Williams, Charles Olson is the main contemporary source for the development of common speech in postmodernist poetry. In his celebrated 1950 essay, "Projective Verse," he elaborates on Pound's and Williams's argument for common speech by concentrating on the importance of bringing the human voice back into contemporary poetry. In an essay that Williams saw fit to quote, Olson declares, "What we have suffered from, is manuscript, press, the removal of verse from its producer and its reproducer, the voice. A removal by one, by two removes from its place of origin and its destination" (*SW*, p. 22). In the style of E. E. Cummings, Olson gained the nuances of the human

26. T. S. Eliot, *On Poetry and Poets*, p. 20.
27. T. S. Eliot, *Selected Essays*, p. 213.

voice by visual effects: he sprinkled his lines about the page, imitating in visual form the pauses and hesitations of speech. Olson argued, "If a contemporary poet leaves a space as long as the phrase before it, he means that space to be held, by the breath, an equal length of time. If he suspends a word or syllable at the end of a line . . . he means that time to pass that it takes the eye—that hair of time suspended—to pick up the next line" (*SW*, pp. 22–23). For example:

> When the attentions change/the jungle
> leaves in
>   even the stones are split
>   they rive   (*N*, p. 3)

With many of his white contemporaries, Baraka has absorbed Olson's formalization of the modernist visual conventions. Baraka has used Olson's ideas to aid him in capturing the sounds of black speech and music in his poetry; Creeley uses them to catch his nervous and staccato speech rhythms; Ginsberg uses them to capture the Niagara of his vatic voice.

The members of the postwar avant-garde were united on the issue of orality. Lawrence Ferlinghetti, a Beat postmodernist, expounded the same theme as Olson when he stated: "The printing press has made poetry so silent that we've forgotten the power of poetry as oral messages. The sound of the street-singer and the Salvation Army speaker is not to be scorned."[28] Not surprisingly, some of Ferlinghetti's most successful poems are his "oral messages" rather than his more formal compositions. Moreover, both Olson and Ferlinghetti found the printing press to be the culprit, demonstrating the second generation's fear of the impersonalizing machine. In response to their fear, both Olson and Ferlinghetti turned their ears to the world: Ferlinghetti, demanding that the poet descend "to the street of the world once more,"[29] chose the figures of the street singer and the Salvation Army speaker to bring home his ideal of a more democratic range of voices in poetry; Olson recorded the

28. The quotation is from the back cover of *A Coney Island of the Mind* (New York: New Directions, 1958).

29. "Populist Manifesto," in *Who Are We Now?*, p. 63.

voices of Gloucester, Massachusetts. Similarly, Jack Kerouac recorded the voices of Lowell, Massachusetts, and the hipsters of New York and San Francisco; Ginsberg the voices of the "best minds of my generation" and his Jewish radical past; Baraka the voices of the Newark Negro and the rhythms of jazz. This democratization of poetic voice grows out of Williams's "the speech of Polish mothers"[30] and Whitman's "I hear America singing, the varied carols I hear"; it stands as a counter to the upper-class voices heard in Eliot's verse. Although Pound, the leading poet of the first generation, was not always comfortable with Whitman, Ginsberg, one of the leading spokesmen of the second generation, considered him the great American poet and innovator. Williams grows out of Whitman; however, he heard America singing through Paterson, New Jersey, a localized America. The contemporary avant-gardists use Williams's localized poetry as a model for their own; that is, they re-create the voices of their poetic neighborhoods.

Baraka's 1959 poetic statement, "How You Sound," begins, "HOW YOU SOUND?? is what we recent fellows are up to" (*N*, p. 424). The recent fellows he refers to are Philip Whalen, Gary Snyder, Michael McClure, Frank O'Hara, Ron Loewinsohn, John Wieners, Robert Creeley, and Ginsberg, that is, the contemporary avant-garde (*N*, p. 425). Moreover, Baraka delineates his poetic descent: "For me, Lorca, Williams, Pound and Charles Olson have had the greatest influence" (*N*, p. 425). The modernists helped Baraka "broaden his Own voice . . . (You have to start and finish there . . . your own voice . . . how you sound)" (*N*, p. 425). Williams, in particular, helped Baraka refine and develop that voice in his own language. Baraka says of Williams in his *Sullen Art* interview (1960) that he learned from him "mostly how to write in my own language—how to write the way I *speak* rather than the way I *think* a poem ought to be written—to write just the way it comes to me, in my own speech, utilizing the rhythms of speech rather than any metrical concept. To talk verse. Spoken verse" (*SA*, p. 80). In a 1970 interview Baraka noted that, before he discovered Williams, "Poetry meant white people . . . I was impressed with white

30. Levertov, *Poet*, p. 254; the subsequent Whitman quotation is from *Leaves of Grass and Selected Prose*, ed. John Kouwenhoven, p. 11.

poetry but I couldn't express myself through that."[31] At college he had read poetry that he found in such paperback anthologies as Oscar Williams's *Poetry of the World* and *Modern Poetry*, which only included white writers; as a result, he thought of poetry as white—"What white men did" (*H*, p. 10). Not having found his own experience reflected in this poetry, his discovery of Williams was pivotal because Williams "was using a language that was still existing."

In the 1970 interview Baraka claims that he rejected white poetry and, finally, the Beats because neither the verse nor its creators spoke in his voice. Yet it was Williams, by example and theory, who taught Baraka how to write in his own language. Baraka realized after reading Williams, "I have my own language . . . we can use our own language and rhythms to recreate these experiences." Williams wrote American; Baraka wrote Afro-American. Consequently, for Baraka, the white avant-garde, in particular Williams, pointed a circuitous route back to blackness, back to self, back to a sense of individual and racial identity.

In *Preface*, Baraka's poetry, influenced by both Olson and Williams and by Baraka's own speaking voice, is virtually indistinguishable from white speech; his quest for his own voice, however, is poignantly evident:

> Then pace the room
> chair to chair, in soft spurts
> (leaving a trail of magazines)—
> it's not desperation. But you got to
> get somewhere? (accent last syllable
> for ethnic identification) & smile.   (p. 14)

Later, Baraka, still following Williams, wrote lines that seek to echo black speech:

> The motherfuckin'
> heart, of the
> motherfuckin'
> day, grows hot
> as a bitch, on her

31. This and the following two quotations come from a 1970 interview of Amiri Baraka conducted by Richard W. Bruner. The tape is housed at the Schomburg Center for Research in Black Culture, New York, New York.

motherfuckin'
way, back home.   (*BMP*, p. 102)

Here Baraka is not writing a new speech but utilizing a different aspect of his own; it would take him years to learn how to incorporate authentic black speech into his work. In his *Autobiography* (1984), he effectively exploits his entire background by writing some sections in black English and others in white, giving readers a chance to experience the shifts of consciousness these changes signal.

Since the postmodernists emphasized the importance of spoken language and produced a poetry based on speech rhythms, they felt the need to read their poetry in public—to escape the silent page—and to discover the music of the human voice—hence the mushrooming of poetry readings in the 1950s to give vent to the individual poet's voice. To place a poet before an audience is to return to the time before print, to the time of oral literature. Furthermore, the nature of poems changed when poets began projecting their meanings through their voices as well as through the written word. For example, Ginsberg, like the ancient bards of preliterate days, wrote chants instead of sonnets, thus expanding the sound range of American poetry. In addition, Ginsberg's chants reach back to Whitman's catalogs, themselves invocatory chants. The black poetry reading grows out of the same rejection of print as did the postmodernist reading, but with important differences. For one thing, the poetry of the blues was more important to the black poet than was the Whitmanesque or ancient chant. In addition, the black poet wanted to address an audience that did not read poetry. To do that, he had to adopt a new style. Larry Neal explains:

> What this has been leading us to say is that the poet must become a performer, the way James Brown is a performer—loud, gaudy and racy. He must take his work where his people are: Harlem, Watts, Philadelphia, Chicago and the rural South. He must learn to embellish the context in which the work is executed and, where possible, link the work to all usable aspects of the music. (*BF*, p. 655)

Ginsberg and Baraka are both great performers with very different styles. Baraka began giving readings in the Beat style but adopted the black, using black vernacular language as well as timbres and patterns from black music. In the poetry reading the sound of his poetry becomes crucial: Baraka almost sings his poems. Significantly, his heirs of the 1960s—Nikki Giovanni and Don L. Lee—also have become great performers. Baraka says he has attempted to make his poetry since the 1960s

> more orally conceived rather than manuscript conceived. The poetry is much more intended to be read aloud, and since the mid-sixties that has been what has spurred it on, has shaped its line. . . . The page doesn't interest me that much—not as much as the actual spoken word. . . . I'm much more interested in the spoken word, and I think that the whole wave of the future is definitely not literary in a sense of books and is tending toward the spoken and the visual. ("HI," p. 27)

One consequence of the poetry reading was to undermine the idea that a poem was something spoken not by a human being but by a persona. The Beat poet was not an actor onstage but someone confessing his life: part of the Beat attack on the mask theory of art was to have a live person saying *I* on a stage. The poetry reading had a psychological aspect as well—it was the forerunner of the encounter group, a way to get in contact with other human beings. When Allen Ginsberg took off his clothes in public, it shocked—serving the traditional avant-garde function of expanding middle-class consciousness—but it also served a symbolic function by signifying that we must be naked before one another; we must remove our masks to find ourselves and to escape the impersonality of the times. Finally, the poetry reading served a communal-ritual function: it was a place where one could belong to a society, a polis, and find shared values. The black poetry reading was designed not to shock the audience but to expand the listeners' consciousness; it was concerned with finding and establishing a community of shared values.

Not just Baraka but also his white confreres considered jazz part of their oral tradition. Many of the writers, especially Kerouac and Ginsberg, used jazz as a model for their literary works. Warren Tallman says of Kerouac's fiction, "Jazz is a dominant influence" (*C*, p. 225). Moreover, Kerouac himself has described his prose style in jazz terms:

> No periods separating sentence-structures already arbitrarily riddled by false colons and timid usually needless commas—but

the vigorous space dash separating rhetorical breathing (as jazz musician drawing breath between outblown phrases)—measured pauses which are the essentials of our speech"—"divisions of the *sounds* we hear"—"Time and how to note it down." (William Carlos Williams). (*C*, p. 66)

Kerouac has also written descriptions of jazz playing that rival Baraka's—especially in *On the Road* (1957). The postmodernists were very much involved with black jazz. They listened to it in coffeehouses and lofts on the lower East Side and in the Village, and their poetry readings were often accompanied by jazz: Kenneth Rexroth and Kenneth Patchen often gave such readings. John Clellon Holms, a Beat writer, wrote *The Horn*, a book about a neglected black jazz saxophonist named Edgar Pool. Baraka was an enthusiast for the new music and introduced it to many members of the white avant-garde, who were inspired by it and tried to capture some of its force in their own medium of expression.

It is likely that the postmodernists, along with earlier black writers such as Ellison and Hughes, provided Baraka with examples of literary uses of jazz. Certainly the fusion of blues elements and open-form technique is evident in "Look for You Yesterday, Here You Come Today," from Baraka's first book, *Preface* (1961). The blues song not only furnishes the title for the poem but also supports the blues mood, "that envious blues feeling" that permeates the entire poem. Unlike Hughes, Baraka gains blues feeling not through directly appropriating blues forms but through mixing blues lyrics with an open form:

> How dumb to be sentimental about anything
> To call it love
> & cry pathetically
> into the long black handkerchief
> of the years.
>> "Look for you yesterday
>> Here you come today
>> Your mouth wide open
>> But what you got to say?" (*P*, p. 17)

Through the use of counterpoint, Baraka creates a poetry that is faithful to the blues feeling but independent of the blues form. The avant-garde gave him the technique to write an open blues poem, and, as we shall see in Chapter 4, as he became disillusioned with the avant-garde his poetry became more and more "jazzy."

Baraka originally turned to the white avant-garde because it provided forms that were original in the way black music was original, and he gained a great deal from his association with the white bohemians. He learned from Williams and Olson to focus on the local; he (not unlike Jean Toomer) gained from the avant-garde flexible techniques for creating an art that could reflect both black language and black forms. Like Toomer, Baraka could capture the quality of black language in his open forms—something that McKay, Cullen, and others could not do in their closed forms. In his poetry Baraka follows three white innovators—he follows Williams and Pound by writing in his own language instead of standard English, and he follows Olson by using visual effects that, imitating the pauses and hesitations of actual speech, help him re-create the black language.

5.

The Williams-Pound-Olson tradition, the radical avant-garde, is didactic, communicative, and political. Both the radical modernists and the postmodernists conceive of poetry as a teaching tool, reject the idea that poetry is autotelic, and feel that poetry has a social function. These positions proved useful to the post-Beat Amiri Baraka. The radical avant-garde tradition from Pound to Ginsberg once again provided the ideas that enabled him to transcend that tradition and helped him become a black artist.

Since the radical avant-garde tradition is didactic, it conceives of poetry as news, that is, as a legitimate source of information about the world. Pound asserted in 1934, "Literature is news that STAYS news."[32] Furthermore, William Carlos Williams, in his beautiful late lyric "Asphodel, That Greeny Flower," declares:

> Of asphodel, that greeny flower
> I come, my sweet,
>   to sing to you!

32. *ABC of Reading*, p. 29.

My heart rouses
    thinking to bring you news
       of something
that concerns you
  and concerns many men. Look at
     what passes for the new.
You will not find it there but in
  despised poems.
     It is difficult
to get the news from poems
  yet men die miserably every day
    for lack
of what is found there.[33]

The assumption here is that the poem is an instrument of information and communication. Pound states, "Language was obviously created, and is, obviously, USED for communication."[34] In "Asphodel," Williams restates the Poundian maxim that "Literature is news that stays news" but with a more dramatic emphasis, claiming that literature contains wisdom and can reveal the nature of reality, providing information that can help the reader live his life. In other words, for Williams literature is a bona fide method of investigation, like physics or sociology, that contributes to our knowledge of reality.

Baraka, following the avant-garde tradition, refers to what one receives from art as information and misinformation: "Let no one convince any black man that he is an American like anybody else. The black writer should be deaf to such misinformation especially since he can prove (vide: Chester Himes' books, Dubois' *Black Reconstruction* or Wright's *Black Boy* and *Native Son*, Franklin Frazier's works, especially *Black Bourgeoise* and *Race and Culture Contacts In the Modern World*, Baldwin's *Native Son* [sic] and *Go Tell It* . . . as staggering for instances) that something quite different is the case" (*H*, p. 165). It is important that Baraka's list of authors who can give information about the black experience includes writers of both "fiction" and nonfiction. By including both novelists, Wright and Baldwin, and social scientists, DuBois

33. *Pictures from Brueghel and Other Poems*, pp. 161–62.
34. Pound, *ABC*, p. 29.

and Frazier, on his list of people who know the truth, Baraka is implying that creative writers as well as nonfiction writers describe the world.

The post-Beat Baraka moved from a symbolist stance, under the influence of Eliot and Yeats, to an objectivist-imagist one, under the influence of Pound and Williams, and became both a didactic and a political poet. Baraka's early poetry has a strong symbolist influence; his first book, *Preface* (1961), is highly symbolist and apolitical; his next, *Dead Lecturer* (1964), struggles to escape symbolism and become political. As happened with other artists, events in the real world influenced Baraka's shift from symbolist to didactic art. For example, among the reasons that led both Pound and Baraka to change from a poetry of aestheticism to a didactic art was their acute perception of human suffering: Pound through the death of close friends in World War I, and Baraka through the wretched conditions of the black masses in America. From Pound to Olson to Ginsberg and Baraka, the objectivist-imagist has seen himself as an unacknowledged legislator of the world. In contrast, the symbolist poet tends to be apolitical because he does not care about this world. In his early symbolist poetry Baraka did not want to present sharp images of the real world; rather, he wanted to suggest, to make personal-subjective statements about his moods, and to celebrate and live in the imagination. In *Preface* he muses, "I dream long bays & towers . . . & soft steps on moist sand. / I become them, sometimes. Pure flight. Pure fantasy. Lean" (p. 26). In the *Dead Lecturer* he strives to chant a new black song that will free the black masses; he wants to live "past my own meekness," past his "quiet verse," to a black didactic art in which the black is "strong in his image of ourselves" (*BMP*, p. 112), strong in a collective black image that will lead to action. Baraka's career could be seen as a struggle between symbol and image, between imagination and reality.

Finally, the Williams-Pound-Olson tradition regards the poet's social function as keeping the public language clear and honest. Pound proclaims emphatically: "Language is the main means of human communication. If an animal's nervous system does not transmit sensations and stimuli, the animal atrophies. If a nation's literature declines, the nation atrophies and decays."[35] The poet's task is to counter the "welter of rhetoric, the diplomat's 'language to conceal thought.' "[36] All the radical avant-gardists, from Pound to the mature Ginsberg to the militant Baraka, are committed to this social function of poetry. For example, Charles Olson uses the true music of poetry to fight the false music (mu-sick) of advertising in "I, Maximus of Gloucester, To You" (1960):

> love is not easy
> but how shall you know,
> New England, now
> the perjorocracy is here, how
> that street-cars, o Oregon, twitter
> in the afternoon, offend
> a black-gold loin?
> . . . .
> how shall you strike,
> o swordsman, the blue-red back
> when, last night, your aim
> was mu-sick, mu-sick, mu-sick
> And not the cribbage game?
> . . . .
> o kill kill kill kill kill
> those
> who advertise you[37]

In the "pejorocracy," Pound's word for the rule of the worst, Emerson's nightmare has become real: "Things are in the saddle, / And ride mankind." For Olson, Pound, and Baraka, the poet's honest music will free man from the corruption of commercial civilization. Revealing his Pound-Olson legacy, Baraka asserts:

> The Black artist . . . is desperately needed to change the images his people identify with, by asserting Black feeling, Black mind, Black judgment. The Black intellectual, in this same context, is needed to change the interpretation of facts toward the Black Man's best interests, instead of merely tagging along reciting white judgments of the world. (*H*, p. 248)

35. Ibid., p. 32.
36. Ibid., p. 33.
37. *The Maximus Poems*, pp. 3–4.

Though each poet has his own agenda—Olson must counter the false mu-sick; Baraka must counter the false white images; and Ginsberg must counter the false magic of the American mass media—all three poets have sought "to produce a new and redeemed man"[38] in America with their didactic poetry.

---

38. Robert Duncan, quoted in Ann Charters's "Introduction" to Olson's *Special View*, p. 11.

3. The Failure of the White Postmodernists

Baraka's art involves more than aesthetic issues: It invariably involves moral values as well. Baraka approvingly quotes the analytic philosopher Ludwig Wittgenstein, who said, "Ethics and aesthetics are one" (*H*, p. 212). The poet adds, "I have always thought of writing as a moral art: that is, basically I think of the artist as a moralist" (*AB*, p. 53). Hence Baraka's turning to the white postmodernists, especially Charles Olson, Allen Ginsberg, Frank O'Hara, and Ed Dorn, was a moral or an ethical as well as an artistic act because in their nonconformism Baraka perceived a moral impulse. But Baraka ultimately saw postmodernist nonconformity as failing to radically challenge prevailing values, and he perceived the failure to be not only an aesthetic one but also a political, ethical, and ethnic one. As a consequence, he turned against the postmodernists. In this chapter I will explore Baraka's perception that the white postmodernists were unable to provide a poetics and a world view that could accommodate his emerging ethics, politics, and ethnicity.

During the late 1950s, Baraka was drawn to the avant-garde because it celebrated the imagination as an inventive faculty that sometimes structures reality, other times creates it. The Beats and New York poets in general brought together aspects of the romantic, surrealist, and symbolist definitions of imagination to create a new definition of their own.[1] Ginsberg, Gregory Corso, Jack Kerouac, John Ashbery, and Frank O'Hara were all committed to an art that sometimes fused dream and mundane worlds, other times fabricated alternative poetic worlds. Most of

1. Somewhat schematically I can say that the romantic imagination structures reality (Kant); the surrealist imagination transports the reader to a higher level of consciousness; the symbolist imagination creates (substitutes) another reality, separate from the real world. The Beats and New York School conflated these various conceptions of the imagination. The Black Mountain Poets were not interested in the creative imagination but instead sought "the apprehension of the absolute condition of present things" (*SW*, p. 47).

these poets sought to escape to worlds of the imagination, to explore new, more adventurous spheres. For Ginsberg, this quest for alternate realities was a quest for expansion of consciousness. Instead of seeking adventure worlds, he sought higher realities. Ashbery's fantasies were an attempt to record the flow of consciousness; O'Hara's and Corso's were a challenge to conventional concepts of sense. By the early 1960s, when he had become painfully aware of politics and human suffering and wanted an art that would be immersed in the real world, Baraka turned against what he then termed the Beat predilection for "fantasy," for dream and chimera.

Nonetheless, the Beats' valorization of the imagination had been one of the things that had attracted Baraka to the avant-garde, and much of his poetry from the Beat years reflects his delight in his new freedom to record his own fantasies. In *Tales* (1967), a group of highly autobiographical stories, he confesses, that while he was growing up, "I lived fantasies in the center of ugly reality . . . where I cd have everything. Where I cd be everything" (p. 93). Moreover, in a 1973 autobiographical essay Baraka states, "The basis of struggle and weight of absolute craziness. (Not madness, but craziness. Like it just wasn't anything real to me. Nothing. Everything was a figment of my imagination. I created it. Thought it up. It wasn't real. And since then my straight and difficult task has been to convince myself that I am actually in the world, and not vice versa)" (*SPP*, p. 195).

In Baraka's psyche there has always been a battle between the imagination and the real world. Baraka was attracted to the world of the imagination because there he could be anyone and have anything he wanted. In his Beat days, the late 1950s and early 1960s, the propensity for fantasy displaced history and ethnicity from his work; feeling kinship with the other Beats, he could say that he was "as any other sad man here / american" (*P*, p. 47). In "In Memory of Radio," a typical Beat poem, he celebrates the imagination:

> Am I a sage or Something?
> Mandrake's hypnotic gesture of the week?
> (Remember, I do not have the healing powers of
>   Oral Roberts . . .
> I cannot, like F. J. Sheen, tell you how to get saved
>   & rich!

I cannot even order you to gaschamber satori like Hitler
   or Goody Knight
. . . .
Saturday mornings we listened to *Red Lantern* & his under-
   sea folk.
At 11, *Let's Pretend*/& we/& I, the poet still do.
   Thank God!   (p. 12)

In this poem Baraka not only valorizes "pretending," he also
rejects the role of poet as an active agent in the world. At that
time Baraka felt that the poet's function was not to save the real
world but to create alternative ones that did not need saving.
This is a tendency of Beat artists. For example, in his 1959 apol-
ogy for his poetry, Ginsberg chides those who want to bring
political reality into poetry:

> A word on the Politicians: my poetry is Angelical Ravings, and
> has nothing to do with dull materialistic vagaries about
> who should shoot who. The secrets of individual imagination—
> which are transconceptual & non-verbal—I mean Unconditioned
> Spirit—are not for sale to this consciousness, are no use to this
> world, except perhaps to make it shut its trap & listen to the
> music of the Spheres.   (C, p. 30)

Baraka's uncollected 1958 poem, "Axel's Castle," probably re-
ferring to both Edmund Wilson's study of French Symbolism
and Villiers de L'Isle-Adam's poetic drama, projects one main
tenet of the Beat aesthetic: that the imagination is more impor-
tant than reality. The hero of the poem lives in an Arthurian
castle in the heart of Greenwich Village:

                    A huge rusty thing.
                    With a roaring moat
                    And red flags strea-
                    Ming from its towers.
        Each evening, after selling his fruit,
        The man dashes out the back door, giggling
        Obscenely, and leaps on his white horse.
        Rushing across the countryside: Across
        Bleecker St. to McDougal, down McDougal
        Till the castle can be seen outlined
        Against the water, stuttering in some
        Effusive glow, like an illuminated trunk.   ("UW," p. 35)

The castle is the dream world, providing a fortress against the mundane.[2] For Beats like Ginsberg and Baraka, the poem could be a fortress against reality. Ginsberg illustrates this inclination when he discusses another avant-garde poet, Gregory Corso, who also rejected the mundane: "A rare goonish knowledge with reality—hip piss on reality also—he prefers his dreams. Why not? His Heaven is Poetry. . . . What a solitary dignitary! He's got the angelic power of making autonomous poems, like god making brooks."[3] Thus Ginsberg boldly declares that the poet no longer has the responsibility to reflect reality in the mirror of art; his only responsibility is to create delightful dreams. Such Beat attitudes nullified the notion that art was the mirror of nature. But unlike other Beat poets, even when Baraka lived in Axel's Castle his dissociation from reality was not total. Despite living in a fairy-tale castle, the protagonist of Baraka's poem knows that the world outside has not disappeared:

> After the meal, the man tells the wife of the big world.
> The cool world. The hard indifferent world of the outside.
> The world of inflationary prices and rotting fruit. ("UW," p. 35)

Unlike Axel—the aristocratic hero of Villiers de L'Isle-Adam's drama—who lets his servants do his living for him, Baraka's middle-class protagonist is not totally separated from reality because economics binds him to it. Similarly, economics also helped draw Baraka out of the world of the imagination—a difficult feat because of his commitment to fantasy. But unlike Gatsby, the self-creating hero of F. Scott Fitzgerald's *The Great Gatsby* (1925), a book Baraka admired, this avant-garde poet wanted to break out of the solipsism of his imagination. He proclaimed, "And reality was the feeling I wanted, and escaped to, from a fantasy world" (*T*, p. 93).

The major reason Baraka sought to exorcise his commitment to imaginary worlds was that during the early 1960s he was forced to come to terms with the reality of contemporary black protest. In a recent interview he reflected, "But I know a lot of what had moved me to make political statements were things in

2. For an excellent reading of Baraka's "Axel's Castle," see Werner Sollors's *Amiri Baraka/LeRoi Jones: The Quest for a "Populist Modernism,"* pp. 15–17.

3. Allen Ginsberg, "Introduction" to Gregory Corso's *Gasoline* (San Francisco: City Lights, 1958), pp. 8–9.

the real world, including poetry that I read, but obviously the civil rights movement upsurge, the whole struggle in the South, Doctor King, SNCC, the Cuban Revolution—all those things had a great deal of influence on me in the late 50s and early 60s" ("HI," p. 24). The historical struggle of black people forced Baraka out of his imaginative refuge and catapulted him into the realm of economics, politics, and race. In *The Dead Lecturer* Baraka declares:

> The poor have become our creators.
>   The black. The thoroughly
> ignorant.   (p. 29)

In this poem Baraka describes how the struggle of the black masses compelled him to re-create himself as a politically engaged artist who had to renounce his apolitical bohemian self. Guilt about the black masses made him rethink his ideas about poetry and the world:

> My own mode of conscience. And guilt, always the obvious
>   connection.
> They [the whites] spread you in the sun, and
>   leave you there, one of a kind, who
>   has no sons to tell this to.   (*DL*, p. 47)

As an avant-garde artist Baraka felt he was a freak, a black who had cut himself off from the black tradition. Moreover, he felt guilty because he had always been a moral being.

Like other black American writers, Baraka perceived that the condition of black people in America calls for the black man to preach for justice. Ralph Ellison even suggested that this is the black man's duty. In the epilogue to *Invisible Man* (1952), the protagonist, mulling over his grandfather's last words, wonders if the old man had meant that "we had to take the responsibility for all of it, for the men as well as the principle because we were the heirs who must use the principle because no other fitted our needs? Not for the power or for vindication, but because we, with the given circumstance of our origin, could only thus find transcendence?"[4] Here, the "principles" are those America was supposed to have been founded on: liberty and equality. Ellison argues that blacks must fulfill the ideals that whites have failed

4. *Invisible Man*, p. 561.

to fulfill. From at least David Walker (1785–1830) on, the black preacher has argued this position; the U.S. Constitution is as holy as the Bible to the black tradition. During the early sixties, Baraka, acknowledging his connection with the black masses, assumed the preacher's role, realizing as he did that he could not live in a world of art for art's sake any longer. It seemed to him that he had to exorcise the avant-garde poetics and world view and find one more consonant with his new imperatives. Metaphorically, he had to move out of Axel's Castle. During the 1960s, Baraka searched for a new black art based on black life. In "Rhythm & Blues," from *The Dead Lecturer* (1964), he portrays the avant-garde poetics and world view as inadequate for the black artist:

> Such act as would give us legend, "This is the man
> who saved us
> Spared us from the disappearance of the sixteenth note, the
> destruction
> of the scale. This is the man who against the black pits of
> despairing genius
> cried, "Save the Popular Song."   (*DL*, p. 46)

As this poem declares, Baraka does not want to be remembered as the black man who saved the West. Here, the sixteenth note and the scale symbolize Western art; metaphorically, Baraka wants to create a new black music rather than save the old white one. When Baraka lauded Coltrane's "murder" of the popular song he implied his own aesthetic: John Coltrane is a great and beautiful philosopher because he destroys Western forms. Coltrane practices the jazz aesthetic on the white popular tune by repeating it and then transforming it. For Baraka, the white avant-garde artist came to represent the antithesis of what Coltrane represented, for the white artist—no matter how rebellious—implicitly affirmed *the* Western tradition. Consequently, in an act of poetic parricide Baraka emulated Coltrane to escape his white role. In "Rhythm & Blues," he declares:

> I am deaf and blind and lost and will not again sing your
> quiet verse. I have lost
> even the act of poetry, and writhe now for cool horizonless
> dawn.   (*DL*, p. 47)

These lines describe a time of spiritual crisis, when Baraka felt that he had lost his moorings in the white world. Finding white poetry, "quiet verse," totally inadequate for his poetic needs, he desperately sought new forms:

> The
> shake and chant, bulled electric motion, figure of what
>   there will be
> as it sits beside me waiting to live past my own meekness.
>   My own light skin.   (*DL*, p. 47)

For Baraka to sing again he would have to take on black forms such as the "shake and chant," which would require him to be brave, to live past his meekness into a new artistic role that declared and affirmed his ethnicity. The poem continues, seeking mighty and vital black creations:

> Bull of yellow perfection, imperfectly made, im-
>   perfectly
> understood, except as it rises against the
>   mountains, like sun
> but brighter, like flame but hotter. There will be
> those
> who will tell you it will be beautiful.   (*DL*, p. 47)

The rising bull of this passage is a recurring symbol for the black, the ethnic, self. The bull suggests the spirit of the new black art, an art that black people—"there will be those"— would find beautiful because it would be an ethnic art, a post-white form.

In addition to determining a new poetic course for himself, after he started facing "hard facts," reality, Baraka battled with Allen Ginsberg about the uses of the avant-garde imagination. Ginsberg's spiritual politics—a politics that tries to change the world through imaginative and spiritual means—came to represent the Beat imagination for Baraka, an imagination aesthetically uplifting but practically useless. In Baraka's new vision, Ginsberg's "Wichita Vortex Sutra" (1966) illustrates the failure of the avant-garde imagination to deal with political reality because Ginsberg did not call for an active, physical—that is, *real*— revolution; rather, he trusted that a revolution of the spirit would effect his ends. In the poem Ginsberg declares:

I call all Powers of imagination
  to my side in this auto to make Prophecy,
                              all Lords
      of human kingdoms to come
. . . .
              & holymen I chant to—
                  Come to my lone presence
                    into this Vortex named Kansas,
    I lift my voice aloud,
      make Mantra of American language now,
        pronounce the words beginning my own millennium,
          I here declare the end of the WAR![5]

For Baraka, Ginsberg epitomized the failure of the white avant-garde imagination to recognize its social and political responsibilities. At this point, Baraka had found the condition of black people too serious to entrust to mystics. In the poem "Western Front," Baraka attacks Ginsberg's spiritual politics/poetics when he asserts:

                              Poems are made
    by fools like Allen Ginsberg, who loves God, and went to India
    only to see God, finding him walking barefoot in the street,
    blood sickness and hysteria, yet only God touched this poet,
    who has no use for the world.   (*BMP*, p. 81)

As Charles Altieri points out, "Ginsberg's 'Wichita Vortex Sutra' . . . so accepts Eastern idealism that it equates abolishing war in one's head with the claim that the Vietnam War has been literally transcended."[6] Altieri's response is, of course, very "Western"; he gives no credence to the possibilities of spiritual revolutions. He seems, moreover, to ignore the poem's theme: the attempt to replace corrupt language with true poetic language. Nevertheless, Altieri articulates a stance identical to Baraka's. Ginsberg's political poetics, then, is the opposite of Baraka's black poetics, and Baraka's attack on Ginsberg was part of his own transformation into a political poet. Within the larger historical context, that is, within the debate among blacks over strategies to achieve their goals, Baraka sided with those who

5. *Planet News*, pp. 126–27.
6. *Enlarging the Temple*, p. 131.

opposed nonviolence. "Non-violence, as a theory of social and political demeanor concerning American Negroes, means simply a continuation of the *status quo*," he remarks in "What does nonviolence mean?" (*H*, p. 144).

In the poem "Black Art" (first published in the *Liberator*, 1966) Baraka declares, "poems are bullshit unless they are / teeth or trees or lemons piled / on a step" (*BMP*, p. 116). For the new Baraka the black poem had to be an active agent, not a vehicle of escape to "another world." Yet even here Baraka's apparent rejection is only partial. In rejecting Ginsberg's otherworldly poetics he employs the techniques and poetics of the imagist-objectivist tradition. Like the imagists-objectivists, Baraka wanted to place real objects in his poems. His intent, however, was radically different from that of his predecessors. While Williams and Pound, for instance, wanted to place real objects in their poems because their antisymbolist stance mandated re-creation of the things themselves, Baraka wanted to place real objects in his poems to create a black world that would reflect the lives of black people.

> We want a black poem. And a
> Black World.
> Let the world be a Black Poem
> And Let All Black People Speak This Poem
> Silently
> or LOUD   (*BMP*, p. 117)

Baraka wanted concrete images in his poems so that his black readers would recognize themselves and be inspired to revolt against their circumstances. Throughout the period when he changed from a Beat to a political poet, Baraka used objectivist techniques to signal the need to destroy the white world:

> We want "poems that kill."
> Assassin poems, Poems that shoot
> guns.   (*BMP*, p. 116)

Interestingly, Baraka's anger brought a response from the poet against whom it was directed; in the long poem *Ankor-Wat* written during 1963, although not published until 1968, Ginsberg acknowledges that Baraka is right about his spiritual politics:

> Nothing but a false Buddha afraid of
>   my own annihilation, Leroi Moi—
> afraid to fail you yet terror those Men
>   their tiger pictures and uniforms
> . . . .
> Leroi I been done you wrong
> I'm just an old Uncle Tom in disguise all along
>   afraid of physical tanks.[7]

Here, Ginsberg openly admits that the source of his spiritual
politics is fear of pain, *physical* pain. Although Ginsberg later
demonstrated real courage in his quest to revolutionize Ameri-
can consciousness—he did, after all, try to bring his moral
stance to bear on the Chicago community with all its violence
in 1968—*Ankor Wat* is a poem about fear. In 1963–1965, when he
was writing the poems in *Black Magic*, Baraka saw Ginsberg's
spiritual politics as an evasive device to protect him from the
bloody political battlefield where Baraka hungered to be, and
Baraka's attack on Ginsberg signaled his own decision to be-
come an active political leader. In sum, in the late 1950s Baraka
was drawn to the white avant-garde in part because its celebra-
tion of the imagination reflected his own valorization of fantasy.
As he became more and more involved in the world of black
politics and the economic and social reality, however, he had to
reconsider the importance of the creative imagination.

Baraka's 1960 trip to Cuba provided him with an alternative
both to the avant-garde and to liberal politics. This trip was one
of the transforming experiences of his life. Clearly, the Cuban
revolution provided him with an alternative he could not find
in America; when he returned from Cuba he had shifted from
being a Beatnik with a little political curiosity—enough, cer-
tainly, to make him take the trip—to being a nascent third-world
revolutionary. While in Cuba he was attacked for his "bourgeois
individualist" stance and defended himself by saying, "Look,
why jump on me? I'm in complete agreement with you. I'm a
poet . . . what can I do? I write, that's all, I'm not even interested
in politics" (*H*, p. 42). Jaime Shelley, a Mexican poet, responded
to him: "You want to cultivate your soul? In that ugliness you

7. *Ankor-Wat,* not paginated.

live in, you want to cultivate your soul? Well, we've got millions of starving people to feed, and that moves me enough to make poems out of" (*H*, pp. 42–43). Struck by this third-world attack on his North American poetics, Baraka began to reevaluate his poetic values. Although it took the political upheavals and struggles of the 1960s in America to make him a full-scale political poet, this period gave birth to the idea of incorporating politics—radical politics—into his poetry; it also gave birth to his disillusionment with postmodernist politics and poetics. The Cuban revolution in its early stages was also inspiring to Baraka because it was an ideal for his emerging revolutionary ideas. Unlike their jaded counterparts in America, who disdainfully stood apart from the American political and social process, Baraka found that the young and energetic intellectuals in Cuba were actually engaged in government and were involved in the process of transforming their country into a more humane place. Soon after his trip he asserted, "Bankrupt utopia sez tell me / no utopias. I will not listen" (*BMP*, p. 38). Now, when the white American avant-garde said that there are no utopias, the new Baraka refused to listen because he had seen utopia—a working radical humanist state. Baraka's trip to Cuba did not provide the model for his new political poetry; however, it did provide the new consciousness that led him to become a third-world artist.

Baraka's friends Allen Ginsberg and Edward Dorn had not gone to Cuba in the early 1960s (Ginsberg had visited during the Batista regime, in 1954, and would visit again, in 1965; neither visit was a success) and did not have the growing pressure of witnessing the mistreatment and revolt of their people. Perhaps because they escaped these pressures, they created an apolitical art. Even Charles Olson is not a politically active artist. Olson complained about the commercialization of America, but, even though he tried to establish an ideal community, a polis, he never really had an audience beyond a few artists and bohemians. Baraka's correspondence with Dorn gives a good picture of the political climate of the early 1960s. In a letter of 10 October 1961, Dorn responds to Baraka's attack on his lack of politics, "Come on, back off. I'm no fucking counter-anything. I'm as truly gassed as anyone, but more embarrassed than others, at the poor prospects of fellow poets singing the praises of any thing so venal as a state."[8] Dorn's is the typical "enlightened" political position of the period, and Baraka attacks it:

> If my letter re your poem sounded crusadery and contentious I'm sorry. But I have gone deep, and gotten caught with images of the world, that exists, or that will be here ever after WE go. I have not the exquisite objectivity of circumstance. The calm precise mind of Luxury. Only we, on this earth, can talk of material existence as just another philosophical problem. . . . "Moral earnestness" (if there be such a thing) ought [to] be transformed into action. (You name it.) I know we think that to write a poem, and be Aristotle's God is sufficient. But I can't sleep. And I do not believe in all this relative shit. There is a right and a wrong. A good and a bad. And it's up to me, you, all of the so called minds, to find out. It is only knowledge of things that will bring this "moral earnestness."[9]

With the phrase "but I have gone deep, and gotten caught with images of the world" we see the political implications of the objectivist-imagist tradition. That is, images of the real world, added to a moral imperative, lead to political art. And after one finds the truth of the real world one is obliged to act. Baraka declares: "We must be in the real world. We must be actual Doers" (*R*, p. 101). He wants action, and he associates action with blackness and inaction with whiteness. In *Tales* (1967) he categorizes: "The straight ahead people, who think when that's what's called for, who don't when they don't have to. Not the Hamlet burden, which is white bullshit, to always be weighing and measuring and analyzing and reflecting. The reflective vs. the expressive. Mahler vs. Martha and The Vandellas. It's not even an interesting battle" (p. 96). The letter to Dorn reveals great pain about the human condition; it shows Baraka rejecting relativism. He wants an absolute—that is why he was drawn to Dante: "Lovely Dante at night under his flame taking heaven. A place, a system, where all is dealt with . . . as is proper" (*SD*, p. 99).

Baraka's poetic parricide was not an easy personal act. Even though he was becoming disillusioned with the white avant-

8. Dorn to Baraka, 10 October 1961 (Dept. of Special Collections, University Research Library, UCLA).

9. Baraka to Dorn, [14–21] October 1961 (Lilly Library, Indiana University).

garde in the early sixties, he could not break away from it, and the result was self-hatred: "I am inside someone / who hates me" (*DL,* p. 15). Much later, he reflected,

> The poetry of that period was still definitely relying heavily on the Creeley-Olson thing. But, while the Creeley-Olson thing is still there in the poetry's form, the content was trying to aggressively address the folks around me, the people that I worked with all the time, who were all Creeley-Olson types, people who took an antipolitical or apolitical line (the Creeley types more so than Olson's followers—Olson's thing was always more political). I was coming out saying that I thought that their political line was wrong. A lot of the poetry in *The Dead Lecturer* is speaking out against the political line of the whole Black Mountain group, to which I was very close . . . [in fact] . . . the overwhelming line [of the entire post–World War II avant-garde] was always anti-political. Or, when politics did emerge, as in Olson's work, I didn't agree with it.[10]

One sign of his distress is that he began to use the word *friends,* which refers to his white avant-garde associates, both ironically and ambiguously. The most shocking use of the term is in the powerful "Black Dada Nihilismus" when he commands the black emanation to

> Rape the white girls. Rape
> their fathers. Cut the mothers' throats.
> Black dada nihilismus, choke my friends   (*DL,* p. 62)

The source of Baraka's ambivalence was his recognition that to be a useful black political artist he had to escape the white world view and poetics; yet he still felt drawn to this white bohemian world and the great ideas of the Western humanist tradition. His ambivalence is reflected in his meditation on Sartre, who had represented everything that he saw as good in the West:

> From Sartre, a white man, it [the West] give
> the last breath. And we beg him die,
> before he is killed.   (*DL,* p. 63)

Baraka's ambivalence about the philosopher stems from their similarities; ironically but not surprisingly, their evaluations of

10. Kimberly W. Benston, "Amiri Baraka: An Interview," *Boundary 2,* 6, no. 2 (Winter 1978), p. 306.

the West differ only in perspective. That is, Sartre's indictment of the West reflects a white perspective, Baraka's a black. Keeping that difference in mind, it is easy to see how their ideas are interchangeable; in his most militant black nationalist state Baraka could have written the following:

> Let us look at ourselves, if we can bear to, and see what is becoming of us. First, we must face that unexpected revelation, the strip-tease of our humanism. There you can see it, quite naked, and it's not a pretty sight. It was nothing but an ideology of lies, a perfect justification for pillage; its honeyed words, its affectation of sensibility were only alibis for our aggressions. . . . You can see it's the end; Europe is springing leaks everywhere. What then has happened? It simply is that in the past we made history and now it is being made of us. The ratio of forces has been inverted; decolonisation has begun; all that our hired soldiers can do is to delay its completion.[11]

Enamored of the Western tradition, Baraka struggled to tear himself from a love that he felt paralyzed him. In fact, paralysis is a major theme of much of his pre–black nationalist poetry. To escape it he had to act:

> Let the combination of morality
> and inhumanity
> begin.   (*DL*, p. 29)

Here Baraka brutalizes himself to achieve the higher goal of black liberation.[12] He had to harden himself to the white avant-garde to become a black revolutionary artist. That this was not an easy task is attested to in much of the poetry in the volumes between *The Dead Lecturer* (1964) and *Black Art* (1966); these are poems of struggle and pain that exhibit the self-dehumanization demanded of one who seeks to destroy an old order of which he or she is a part. It is increasingly clear that all groups who have been oppressed by the society in which they have found themselves must go through some kind of self-brutalizing process

11. Jean Paul Sartre, "Preface" to Frantz Fanon's *The Wretched of the Earth*, pp. 21, 23.
12. For a further discussion of Baraka's self-brutalization, see Sollors's discussion of Baraka's anti-Semitism, *Amiri Baraka/LeRoi Jones*, pp. 198–200. Sollors argues: "Baraka's anti-Semitism was . . . an intensely personal exorcism of his own past, and his anti-Semitic references included his former wife and literary milieu in New York" (p. 199).

before they can find a voice of their own. Unlike parricide, where they kill the father, here they must murder the image that the father/society has implanted within their own psyches. For instance, Joseph P. Lash has observed, "Virginia Woolf confessed that to be a writer she had to begin by killing that part of herself which put a man's views before her own." In *The Death of the Moth* (1942), Woolf asserts:

> Had I not killed her she would have killed me. She would have plucked the heart out of my writing. For, as I found, directly I put pen to paper, you cannot review even a novel without having a mind of your own, without expressing what you think to be the truth about human relations, morality, sex."[13]

The part that Woolf is killing corresponds to the Victorian idealization of the angel in the house, the woman too good, too selfless, to confront the world on its own terms. Similarly, in Baraka's play *The Slave* (1964), the hero Walker Vessels, must kill the love of whites in himself before he can become a black revolutionary.[14]

For Baraka to escape his own guilt, he had to find another mode of art more appropriate for the black masses. In the poetry of this period (1961–1965) we see Baraka's desperate attempt to exorcise the white world from himself:

> I don't love you. Who is to say what that will mean.
>   I don't
> love you, expressed the train, moves, and uptown, days
>   later
> we look up and breathe much easier
>
> I don't love you   (*BMP*, p. 55)

Here Baraka tries the magic spell of "I don't love you" to tear himself from his white friends downtown. The subway expresses movement, movement away from his psychic paralysis, uptown to his active, revolutionary black self. In "Citizen Cain"

13. The Joseph P. Lash quotation is from his review of Anne Morrow Lindbergh's *War Within and Without, The New York Times Book Review,* 20 April 1980, p. 24. The Virgina Woolf quotation is from her *Death of the Moth and Other Essays* (Harcourt, Brace, Jovanovich, 1970), p. 238.

14. See *Dutchman and The Slave,* pp. 66–67. The passage does not lend itself to short quotation.

Baraka explores the need to escape his old life and find a new one:

> Roi, finish this poem, someone's about to need you, Roi,
> dial the mystic number, ask for holy beads . . .
> . . . .
> Work out your problems
> like your friends on some nice guy's couch. Get up and hit
> someone like you useta. Don't sit here trembling under the
> hammer. Fate like a season of abstract reference. Like an
> abstract execution where only ideas are shot full of holes.
> Don't sit there drowned in your own bad writing. Get up and
> throw that ball. Move your hips, cut, like the white boys,
> for ten more yards. . . .
> . . . .
> Ask the white man
> for your passport and quit it, little jesus. Your time is up
> in this particular feeling. In this particular throb of meaning.
> Roi, baby, you blew the whole thing.   (*BMP*, p. 8)

The poem presents Baraka's realization that if he is going to be a black revolutionary artist he cannot be like his white friends. Unlike them, he cannot work out his problems on a psychiatrist's couch because his problems are more than personal in nature—they are political and, therefore, communal. Strongly feeling this, he can no longer escape the world by writing bad poetry—that is, poetry defined by his evolving black standards, subjective poetry not committed to political action. Like a football player he must move to action and out of the world of mere abstract ideas, the bohemian world, "where only ideas are shot full of holes." In the closing lines Baraka prepares to leave the white world and its vision of reality.

In *Preface* (1961) Baraka did not question his affiliation with the white avant-garde; rather, as a racial outsider he identified with those socially outside the American mainstream. However, by the time of *The Dead Lecturer* (1964), he had found that the avant-garde was politically not extreme enough; hence his characterization of them as liberals. In "A Dark Bag" (1963), a literary piece, Baraka clarified what he meant by liberal:

> This review or chronicle might be my last liberal, or not-literal, act, unless quite soon there busts within me an enormous gland of misplaced and not wholly unsentimental regard for the social

malaise that so willingly shapes (and has for the last thirty years shaped) the flexibly official political/cultural tone of this society's complete retreat into fantasy and self-destruction. I mean I hope it is my last personal gesture of "adjustment" in the direction of a burning building. . . . So let this also serve as a loud cry for the firemen, or whatever other realists there may be in the area. Possibly the fire is real. (*H*, p. 121)

Baraka's definition of "liberal" action as a "non-literal act" implies that it is action manifested only in words. By this time, Baraka wanted poems to act directly in the world. In "A Poem Some People Will Have to Understand," Baraka explains:

> We have awaited the coming of a natural
> phenomenon. Mystics and romantics, knowledgeable
> workers
> of the Land.
> But none has come.
> (Repeat)
>   but none has come.
> Will the machine gunners please step forward?   (*BMP*, p. 6)

In this poem the "people who would have to understand" are the white liberals, Baraka's old "friends"; they would have to understand that violence would occur because the usual liberal channels had not effected any change in the condition of black people. In fact, the liberals are ironically labeled mystics and romantics to emphasize their ineffectualness in the social realm. Finally, it is clear, the only avenue left for Baraka was violence: "Let the dada machine gunner step forward!"

In 1961, in "Letter to Jules Feiffer," Baraka said of the liberal point of view,

> The new countries of Asia, Africa, and Latin America are not interested in your shallow conscience-saving slogans and protests of moderation or "political guarantees." As a character in Burroughs' *Naked Lunch* says, "You think I am inarrested in contracting your horrible ol' condition? I am not inarrested at all." (*H*, p. 65)

Clearly, Cuba changed Baraka's political consciousness; as he formulates third-world necessities here, they differ so radically from America's necessities that solutions proposed by white Americans are irrelevant. But, even though Cuba changed Baraka from a rebel (someone who is discontented with his society but does not try to overthrow it) into a third-world revolutionary (someone who is trying to overthrow his society and its vision of reality), he did not immediately identify with the third world. He retained his identification with the West in the midst of his new sympathies:

> We are an old people already. Even the vitality of our art is like bright flowers growing up through a rotting carcass.
> But the Cubans, and the other new peoples (in Asia, Africa, South America) don't need us, and we had better stay out of their way. (*H*, p. 62)

Baraka did not find his new vitality, cease being the dead lecturer, until he became a third-world poet who, vigorously alive in his new black skin, could say, "We wear the Life sign, the ankh" (*R*, p. 19).

M. L. Rosenthal, though not a contemporary avant-gardist, in his essay "American Poetry Today" (1973) illustrates the same failings of the liberal imagination as the bohemians. Rosenthal understands that Baraka's work embodies the politics of confrontation: however, he does not recognize the need to act out racial confrontation. He observes that many of Baraka's poems "are the deliberate invention of an intellectual poet setting out to internalize the violence of the poor black's experience and convert it into an equal and opposite reaction, and one just about as acceptable as a promise of national enlightenment."[15] Rosenthal rejects Baraka because Baraka rejects the liberal dream. He focuses on Baraka's call for violent revolution and ignores Baraka's radical idealism and utopian dreams. Furthermore, Rosenthal refuses to understand the personal agony Baraka felt at being cut off from his people; he refuses to recognize Baraka's need for ethnic solidarity. In claiming that Baraka was pretending to be someone he was not (a poor illiterate black) while, ironically, Baraka was actually trying to stop pretending to be someone he was not (an "imitation white boy," a gray assimilated American intellectual), Rosenthal distorts Baraka's intentions to fit his own white, liberal world view.

It is not enough to argue, as Rosenthal does that canonically respectable figures like Shakespeare and Shelley argued hon-

15. M. L. Rosenthal, "American Poetry Today," pp. 61–64.

estly in their art; we must be able to evaluate, fairly, the arguments of living poets as well, to examine the reasons they act, and speak, as they do. Rosenthal wants to sit down at the negotiating table with a political poet for whom conversation was only a prelude to violence. In fact, Clay, the protagonist of *Dutchman* (1964), says to a white that when blacks learn to imitate Western culture, "They'll murder you, and have very rational explanations. Very much like your own. They'll cut your throats, and drag you out to the edge of your cities so the flesh can fall away from your bones, in sanitary isolation" (*DS*, p. 36). Rosenthal believes that talk can still bring results; Baraka believes the only answer is violence. Once Western rationalism failed Baraka, he espoused dada violence and sought an art that could absorb black radical politics. To achieve this new black art he continued to kill Crow Jane, the white muse that he had created from the suggestiveness of Yeats's Crazy Jane: "Crow Jane, Crow Jane, don't hold your head so high, / You realize, baby, you got to lay down and die" (*DL*, p. 48) sings Mississippi Joe Williams. In the fifth movement of "Crow Jane" Baraka kills Crow Jane, the white muse, "Erect / . . . for that lady, a grave of her own . . . The lady is dead" (*DL*, p. 53).[16] Commenting on the poem, Baraka has said,

> The Western aesthetic dies . . . at least my use for it. That whole book, *The Dead Lecturer,* is really about that: The moving away from the whole Western aesthetic. . . . She [Crow Jane] has been used by an Afro-American, i.e., me. And I know she has got to be killed off because there is no further use—I can't get anything else from her. ("HI," p. 26)

Baraka was greatly disturbed at what he perceived to be the failure of the postmodernists to provide a poetics flexible enough to include black language and culture, although, as this study shows, it had not included black language and culture only because no one before Baraka had seen that as an imperative. Baraka himself became the postmodernist who extended avant-garde poetics to reflect black ethnic and political realities. In essence ethnicity was excluded from the post–World War II

16. For a helpful discussion of the influence of Yeats's Crazy Jane on Baraka's Crow Jane, see Kimberly Benston's *The Renegade and the Mask,* pp. 115–19.

poem: the language of the majority culture dominated the avant-garde poem of the 1960s. From a minority perspective, it was written in the language of another tribe and, furthermore, was larded with that tribe's values and assumptions about reality. In short, the white avant-garde failed to provide a ready-made medium for Baraka's emerging ethnic experience. Baraka comments: "I was consciously striving for a post-bourgeois/Western form, even before the cultural nationalist period. Now, Creeley, Olson, et al. were themselves post-bourgeois/academic poets, and that was valuable for me. But they were also, in some ways, an extension of Western art."[17] More bluntly, Baraka asserts: "The Village was frustrating because these people could not do what I wanted; they could not create a black literature. It had nothing to do with them."

I think it would be instructive to quote the following "cultural nationalist" statement without first identifying the militant author:

> The language in which we are speaking is his before it is mine. How different are the words home, Christ, ale, master, on his lips and mine! I cannot speak or write these words without unrest of spirit. His language, so familiar and so foreign, will always be for me an acquired speech. I have not made or accepted its words. My voice holds them at bay. My soul frets in the shadow of his language.[18]

The author is James Joyce, and the passage is from *A Portrait of the Artist as a Young Man* (1916); it illustrates the universal nature of minority artists' struggles with majority cultures. The Irish must speak English because the English are the masters. Even though the young hero, Stephen Dedalus, is fluent in English, it remains a foreign and uncomfortable tongue for him because it is the language of the colonizer of his people. For Joyce, to speak this foreign language is to betray one's own tongue, culture, and values. In light of the above, it is not surprising that Baraka often uses the Irish example when he is discussing ethnic expression:

17. "Benston Interview," p. 308. The immediately following quotation is from "Schomburg Interview," conducted by Richard W. Bruner (1970).

18. James Joyce, *A Portrait of the Artist as a Young Man* (New York: The Viking Press, 1956), p. 189. For an excellent discussion of Irish and black literature, see C. L. Innes's "Language in Black and Irish Nationalist Literature," *The Massachusetts Review* 16, no. 1 (Winter 1975): 77–91.

"If you think about Irish literature, from Wilde on, and if you think of Wilde, Shaw, Yeats, Joyce, Synge, O'Casey, Beckett—if you think about this, those people are Irish, they are not English; and those men have been the strength of English literature for a long time" (*AB*, p. 61). Frantz Fanon, too, recognized the significance of language for a colonized people:

> To speak means to be in a position to use a certain syntax, to grasp the morphology of this or that language, but it means above all to assume a culture, to support the weight of a civilization. . . . The Negro of the Antilles will be proportionately whiter—that is, he will become closer to being a real human being—in direct ratio to his mastery of the French language. Every colonized people . . . finds itself face to face with the language of the civilizing nation; that is, with the culture of the mother country."[19]

In America black culture is a subculture, and Baraka, like Joyce's protagonist, tried to escape the influence of the ruling culture. Contending that the dominant culture controls the lives of the minority, Baraka took the idea of the Afro-Americans as a colonized people seriously. During the late 1950s and early 1960s, he assumed that an unmodified white avant-garde would provide forms and methods that would free him from the colonizer's language and ideas, but by the midsixties he had come to realize that the avant-garde shared ideas and values with the colonizer and that the only way the avant-garde could be useful to him was if he himself took its forms of revolt and adapted them to the black situation. Moreover, he came to see white avant-garde culture as dangerous to the ethnic artist. Baraka states, "The culture of the powerful is very infectious for the sophisticated, and strongly addictive. To be any kind of 'success' one must be fluent in this culture. Know the words of the users, the semantic rituals of power. This is a way into wherever it is you are not now, but wish, very desperately, to get into" (*H*, p. 169). With his middle-class speech and background, Baraka found it easy to write white verse that exhibited white assumptions, but in doing so he risked the total loss of ethnic identity in the act of becoming an artist. In 1966 Baraka confessed, "Having read all of whitie's books, I wanted to be an

19. *Black Skin, White Masks* (New York: Grove Press, 1969), pp. 17–18.

authority on them. Having been taught that art was 'what white men did,' I almost became one, to have a go at it" (*H*, p. 10). And the hero of *The System of Dante's Hell* (1965) cries out: "Please, you don't know me. Not what's in my head. I'm beautiful. Stephen Dedalus. A mind, here where there is only steel. Nothing else. Young pharaoh under trees. Young pharaoh, romantic, liar. Feel my face, how tender. My eyes. My soul is white, pure white, and soars" (p. 140).

For the Baraka of the midsixties, to be an artist was to be white, to be cut off from ethnicity. To write was to be universal, which, for him as for other minority artists, also meant to be white. Dudley Randall amusingly illustrates this theme in "Black Poet, White Critic":

> A critic advises
> not to write on controversial subjects
> like freedom or murder,
> but to treat universal themes
> and timeless symbols
> like the white unicorn.
> *A white unicorn?*[20]

For Baraka, as for Randall, the white critic's preoccupation with the universal and the timeless was irrelevant to black art. A white unicorn, a symbol of white presumption, is simply extraneous to either black life or black art.[21] In the Beat world, Gregory Corso, the poet, illustrated how crude "the white critic" could be when he earnestly told Baraka, "Black writers are stuck because they're always talking about their people" (*H*, p. 163). And Baraka replied, "But who does anyone talk about? Hemingway is always talking about his people, or Joyce. What does anyone think The Dubliners were—abstract literary categories? It is simply, that someone is trying to tell you write is white" (*H*, p. 163). But there were subtler forms of anti-ethnic bias in the white avant-garde. In a 1965 essay the avant-garde critic Kenneth Rexroth said of Baraka:

20. *The Black Poets*, ed. Dudley Randall (New York: Bantam Books, 1971), p. 33.
21. During Baraka's Beat stage, he wrote at least one poem about unicorns: "The Gift of the Unicorn," *Epos* 10, no. 2 (Winter 1958): 14.

For a number of years LeRoi Jones was the most significant Negro poet to come up since Jean Toomer. His first two books contain poetry which is moving, penetrating and independent of race, except as a given factor of the poet's situation. In recent years he has succumbed to the temptation to become a professional Race Man of the most irresponsible sort. Coming as he does from middle-class suburbia, his attitude is indistinguishable from Senator Eastland's image of the Negro, and differs only in that he approves enthusiastically of this artifact. His loss to literature is more serious than any literary casualty of the Second War, a particularly tragic loss to the tradition of Daddy Grace, essentially a White Man's Negro, a kind of Tom Uncleism, a hot commodity for white masochists.[22]

Rexroth saw Baraka's taking on of racist stereotypes but did not understand either his intention or his need to break away from the white world to become himself. And it is strange that Rexroth could read and approve of *Dead Lecturer* without seeing Baraka struggling to find his black self and a new black art.

Similarly, Charles Olson, Baraka's spiritual father, showed a surprising blindness to Baraka's racial imperatives in a letter to Baraka probably written in 1963:

O. K. Simply thoughts on your own position (speaking for the Negro, and being struck all over the place, both in *Blues People* and in the Midstream piece ["What Does Nonviolence Mean?"], on how much you speak of as Negro has been only my own experience likewise—so I am solely persuaded that your position that the Negro solely ought to act as an end and change of what is manifestly no good is in fact any man's who wishes to have had a life in society which was more legitimate.[23]

Olson would not allow a unique role for the black; rather, he insisted that all good men are alike. Refuting such critics in "Philistinism and the Negro Writer" (1966), Baraka argued for ethnic diversity:

I found myself publishing that writing which I thought was the most valuable. Not the writing that reflected those tired white lives again, but necessarily those people, those white and black

---

22. "Poetry in the Sixties," in Rexroth's *With Eye and Ear*, p. 77.
23. Olson to Baraka, n.d. (Simon Fraser University Library).

people who were talking about a side of America that was more valuable because it hadn't been talked about. Allen Ginsberg, who gives the Jewish memory of dissent in this culture, since this culture asks and has asked all immigrants to strip themselves of the very things that would make their own culture valuable, so that the Italian who comes to America becomes an American and the Italian thing is lost. The Jew who gets into America is an American and the Jewishness is lost, and so now they want to break your back, too, Negro, so that when you go into that place, there will be no dissent, there will be no dissent at all, so that you will be faceless, too, and your literature will reflect some kind of tired thirst for, perhaps, luxury and comfortable ignorance. (*AB*, p. 61)

Baraka did not want to lose his ethnicity, did not want to become refined like the nineteenth-century black novelist Charles Chesnutt, who represents, for him, washed-out middle-class black writing. Like the black dada musician, Baraka wanted to keep the funk, the reality, to keep his art crude and real. At first Baraka thought he had found the counterpart of jazz in the white avant-garde tradition, but in the end that tradition turned out not to be "funky" enough. He had to radically alter—even apparently reject—the white avant-garde tradition to find himself.

4. The Transformed Poem ⟋⟍

In Chapter 1 I discussed the jazz transformation process generally and theoretically; in this chapter I will consider the application of that world view by examining specific poems written between the early sixties and 1984. Jazzification, the practical application of the jazz aesthetic to Baraka's poetry, follows two basic patterns: in the first, Baraka inverts uncongenial bourgeois forms and ideas, making them black by turning them into their opposites; in the second, he radically modifies avant-garde notions that he finds congenial but still too "white." In this latter mode, the modification is so extreme that one could call it transmutation. In both patterns Baraka finds the implicit blackness in whatever white mode he is transforming. His radical techniques are infused with an ethnic world view that takes images, poetic techniques, and avant-garde attitudes that are "pure white" and transforms them into a new and distinctively black vision that simultaneously rejects and accepts some of the most sophisticated and radical of his white predecessors' ideas.

1.

Among the first of the "uncongenial" bourgeois forms Baraka recognized and attacked were white bourgeois images and stereotypes of blacks. Believing that popular culture shapes black reality as well as reflecting white middle-class reality, Baraka most often inverts bourgeois forms taken from the world of popular culture. Contemplating images of blacks created by the white imagination has become a way for him to penetrate black reality because he can articulate the way black people have responded to the roles whites have imposed on them. For instance, in "A Poem for Willie Best," from *The Dead Lecturer* (1964), Baraka meditates on the image of the popular film character actor Willie Best (1916–1962), who as Sleep 'n' Eat, a black buffoon, was featured in a number of Hollywood movies of the 1930s and 1940s. Sleep 'n' Eat is a black stereotype created by the white mind. He is

> Lazy
> Frightened
> Thieving
> Very potent sexually
> Scars
> Generally inferior
> > (but natural)
>
> rhythms   (p. 26)

Notwithstanding the degrading stereotypes, for Baraka "This is a literature, of / symbols. And it is his [Willie Best's] gift" (*DL*, p. 20). Here the poet presents the actor as a rebel against his role. Best is more than a figment of the white imagination; he is actually a flesh-and-blood actor behind the white image who has extended his role beyond its white creators' intentions. The black actor, the man, has seized the symbol and reinterpreted it, and the poet both articulates Best's interpretation and furthers the actor's task through reinterpretations of his own. Baraka glosses the poem: "Willie Best presents the black as the minstrel—the black as the bizarre funny person, yet the black as victim, and this black minstrel victim having to come to grips with that—with his victimhood, with his minstrelsy in order to change that" ("HI," p. 25). Here the poet perceives what critic Donald Bogle has noted of black character actors in general: as they "played the roles and found themselves wedged into these categories, the history became one of actors battling against the types to create rich, stimulating, diverse characters."[1]

By inverting this white form, this symbol of the degraded black, Baraka presents the black minstrel as a Christ figure:

> A Cross. The gesture, symbol, line
> arms held stiff, nailed stiff, with
> no sign, of what gave them strength.
> The point, become a line, a cross, or
> the man, and his material driven in
> the ground. If the head rolls back

---

1. *Toms, Coons, Mulattoes, Mammies, and Bucks*, p. 20.

and the mouth opens, screamed into
existence, there will be perhaps
only the slightest hint of movement—
a smear; no help will come. No one
will turn to that station again.   (*DL*, p. 19)

Other writers—most notably Harriet Beecher Stowe—have seen
degraded blacks as Christ symbols, but most have stressed their
passivity while suffering. In contrast, Baraka's black Christ is
not impotent; rather, he seeks revenge for his wrongs. In the
poem, the troubled actor cries out: "I'm tired / of losing. / I got
ta cut 'cha" (*DL*, p. 25). Like the character Clay, in *Dutchman*, in
this inversion of the Sleep 'n' Eat image violence provides an
escape from minstrelsy; the black who is forbidden to express
his pain becomes a potential killer. For Baraka, more than the
mindless clown is implied in Best's portraiture; he is

A renegade
behind the mask. And even
the mask, a renegade
disguise.   (*DL*, p. 26)

In large part, the inversions of Baraka's art, from *Dead Lecturer*
on, are aimed at awakening the potential killer, the revolution-
ary Bigger Thomas, in the submissive black. Exposing or invert-
ing popular images of blacks is important to Baraka because he
believes these images exercise tremendous power over the be-
havior of blacks by providing negative role models. Like Whit-
man, he thinks one function of art is to supply appropriate role
models or (to use Whitman's term) archetypes. Therefore, it is
imperative to him that images of docile blacks, of Uncle Toms,
be replaced by images of heroic blacks, of Malcolm Xs, because
heroic images will inspire heroic behavior. In "A Poem for Black
Hearts" Baraka demands, "black man, quit stuttering and shuf-
fling" and act like Malcolm, "black and strong in his image"
(*BMP*, p. 112).

By restructuring white stereotypes Baraka is trying to ex-
pose the hidden reality of black self-images and to create new
images—postwhite—no longer dependent on white imagery
and capable of communicating black realities without a mask.
Unlike Bessie Smith, who Baraka presents in *Dutchman* as a
paradigm of black artistic masking, Baraka wants the artist

to cast aside coded lyricism. In *Dutchman,* Clay, the protagonist, blurts out:

> If Bessie Smith had killed some white people she wouldn't have needed that music. She could have talked very straight and plain about the world. No metaphors. No grunts. No wiggles. Just straight two and two are four. Money. Power. Luxury. Like that. All of them. Crazy niggers turning their backs on sanity. When all it needs is that simple act. Murder. Just murder! Would make us all sane. (*DS,* p. 35)

As Kimberly W. Benston summarizes Smith's position: "Bessie Smith uses the mask of the blues as a coded language, asking whites to 'kiss my ass' to keep herself from murdering them."[2] In contrast, Baraka is proposing an unadorned art that would talk "straight and plain about the world." Although the title *Hard Facts* only applies to one of Baraka's books, it suggests the direction of all his poetry after *Preface.* He wanted an art of hard facts that would expose the evils of money, power, and luxury and would drive the black sane, that is, into political action that would aid in the destruction of America.

It is clear that image reversal, the process in which Baraka is engaged, has its source in the social world and that Baraka inverts images and ideas in order to "right" them from a black perspective. He wants to change "the public image the white man has fashioned to characterize Black Men [because they are references black men identify with in the West] since that's what is run on them each day by white magic, i.e., television, movies, radio, etc.—the Mass Media (the *Daily News* does it with flicks and adjectives)" (*H,* p. 247). In *Black Magic* (1969) art is used to counter the white magic of the mass media, the imagemakers. And in *Home,* his 1966 collection of essays, Baraka states, "The Black artist . . . is desperately needed to change the images his people identify with, by asserting Black feeling, Black mind, Black judgment" (p. 248). This is a succinct expression of cultural nationalism—that the artist's function is to change the cultural imagery with which his people identify.

The best illustration of Baraka's inversion of white popular images of blacks appears in his 1970 black nationalist drama, *Jello.* In this play—which re-creates the radio/TV world of Jack

2. *Baraka: The Renegade and the Mask,* p. 167.

Benny—the faithful black chauffeur, Rochester, has turned "postuncletom," that is, militant, complete with a natural hair style and a new hip vocabulary. During the course of the play, Rochester does the militant jerk (a black dance associated with revolution and identity), steals his "backpay," and threatens Jack Benny's life. Like the harmless grinning minstrel symbol from *The Slave*, here the comforting stereotype of the black servant has been inverted and made frightening. This Rochester is equipped with a "trusty razor" that he uses to regain what he considers rightfully his. But, while Rochester is revolutionary rather than criminal, Jack Benny—the white man—can only see him as a knife-wielding coon. Describing him to his coperformer, Dennis, he employs the vocabulary whites use to describe (and to categorize) blacks who do not conform to the servant role:

> No, no Dennis, it's not a joke. It's true. Look at Rochester. You never saw him look like that before, did you? All that bushy hair. Look at his horrible eyes. How hard they've gotten . . . and cold. It's no joke Dennis, Rochester, our own dear Rochester, has become a mad thief and murderer. (*J*, p. 28)

Speaking from the white perspective, Benny sees Rochester as "a mad thief and murderer" rather than as a revolutionary black militant. This falsifying imagery protects Benny in that he does not have to confront the real Rochester or try to understand the significance of his change. Most importantly from the black perspective, it places the entire burden of guilt on the manservant. It is difficult to ascertain whether Rochester's eyes have actually turned hard and cold—that is, if Rochester has undergone the hardening of sentiment needed to commit a revolutionary act—or whether Benny's white point of view can only interpret them that way. When Mary, another actor on the show, saunters in, Benny cries out: "No, Mary, this is not the script. This is reality. Rochester is some kind of crazy nigger now. He's changed. He wants everything" (*J*, p. 31). For Benny, "crazy" describes the black who challenges the white hierarchy. Rochester's challenge to Benny is an instrusion of black reality into the white fantasy world much like "mad" Nat Turner's intrusion into the antebellum south. As a representative of White America, Benny does not want to face the crazy nigger's demands, to come to terms with his social significance, to examine the social causes for his bizarre behavior. Baraka has turned Benny's happy nigger upside down, creating a new black figure who will act as a model for revolutionary blacks. And through his art Baraka is trying to create legions of "crazy niggers."

From a far more conservative political position, another black artist, Ishmael Reed, also finds it important to alter popular culture in order to reshape white images of blacks. Both artists recognize the potency of the popular images that dominate the American imagination, whether black or white. Like Baraka, the novelist/satirist Reed wants to establish right conduct and create new heroes. Unlike Baraka, Reed tries to accomplish his ends by poking fun rather than by preaching. Reed does not invert popular images; rather, he reshapes them to fit his narrative and political aims. A glance at Reed's work will show that Baraka is not alone in his demand for the radical reconstruction of white stereotypes of blacks.

In *The Last Days of Louisiana Red* (1974), Reed refashions characters from the "Amos 'n' Andy" show of TV/radio fame. In the novel, Kingfish Stevens and Andy Brown have become "revolutionaries," 1960s militants who, for Reed, are hustlers rather than heroes. According to Kingfish: "They took us off television and radio and gave us freedom to roam the world, unchecked, hustling like we never hustled."[3] Kingfish expresses the spirit of the "revolutionary organization" to which he and Brown belong:

Kingfish: Bro. Brown, let me borry some beer outta your pitcher. Share and share alike is what we Moochers say. (Pours himself a drink.)
Brown: Help yo self, Kingfish, share and share alike as the Moochers say, but sometimes I wonder, Kingfish; look like I'm doing all the sharin.[4]

For Reed, the Moochers represent the radical organizations of the sixties that talked revolution but did not actually change the lot of black people. In passionate response to radical chic solutions to black people's problems, Reed proposes hard work

3. *The Last Days of Louisiana Red*, p. 128.
4. Ibid., p. 53.

to improve the black condition. In *Louisiana Red* "bushwa" Amos/Jones, an industrious character, is the hero, a man who has his creator's approval when he says, "Well, as you know, I gave up working for the taxi company. I now manage a fleet of limousines."[5] In many ways, Ishmael Reed is a hip Booker T. Washington who, though rejecting submissiveness, nonetheless supports black industriousness and self-help. Another spokesman for the author remonstrates with a character modeled on Eldridge Cleaver: "Look at yourself, Street. . . . All you knew how to do was to destroy. Maybe destruction was good then, it showed our enemies we meant business. But we can't continue to be kids burning matches while the old folks are away. We have to buckle down."[6] In the course of the story Kingfish and Andy try to rob "bushwa" Amos, but Amos catches them in the act and calls the police, gun in hand. Unlike Baraka, Reed sees robbery as a crime against the hard-working members of the black community rather than as a revolutionary act. While it is unlikely that Reed would look kindly on Baraka's "postuncle-tom" Rochester, and fairly certain that Baraka would only view Reed's Amos as a Tom, it is important that both authors are committed to the reshaping of black stereotypes. Despite their radical differences about the kinds of heroes who will create their new worlds, both see popular culture as a key to reshaping American attitudes.

In addition to images from popular culture, Baraka also inverts other white images in his search for new black ones. Asserting that whites (rather than blacks) are animals, he commands his black reader to "leave the beast / in its snowy den" (*BMP*, p. 167) and asserts, "To turn their [whites'] evil backwards is to live" (*BMP*, p. 192). Taking the common white stereotype of blacks wielding razors, he forges a new image by adding a significant adjective to indicate that these heroes are defending their people against the oppressor: "thin heroic blades / the razor. Our flail against them" (*SP*, p. 41). In *Black Magic*, written during the cultural nationalist period when reversal of black/white relationships was a major goal, he repeatedly restructured common images of blacks by referring to the

5. Ibid., p. 132.
6. Ibid., p. 107.

blacks as "heroes"; playing with images of Africans projected in
Tarzan movies, he raises them to significance:

> Remembering dances for tarzan
> until the jungle pots
> boil darkness and the hot
> sun fashions it into
> black heroes.   (*BMP*, p. 307)

Certainly one clue to Baraka's inversions lies in the poem that
concludes "State/Meant," the last essay in *Home*. In this poem
his penchant for punning and his quest for new black images
come together in a complex word play:

> We are unfair and unfair
> We are black magicians, black art
> s we make in black labs of the heart.

> The fair are
> fair, and death
> ly white.

> The day will not save them
> and we own
> the night.   (*H*, p. 252)

Here, puns on the meaning of "fair" (both "light-skinned" and
"even-handed"), the suggestion of supernatural black powers
pitted against white impotence, and, most significantly, the
transmutation of Langston Hughes's imagery of day and night
in "Dream Variations" ("To fling my arms wide / In some place
of the sun, / To whirl and to dance / Till the white day is done. /
Then rest at cool evening / Beneath a tall tree / While night
comes on gently / Dark like me"[7]) from the lighthearted to the
ominous, show Baraka militantly inverting black/white relation-
ships in his creation of images that will at once give blacks new
confidence and inspire them to become revolutionaries.

2.

In *The Theory of the Avant-Garde* (1962), Renato Poggioli argues,
"The conventions of avant-garde art, in a conscious or uncon-

---

7. Langston Hughes, *Selected Poems*, p. 14.

scious way, are directly and rigidly determined by an inverse relation to traditional conventions."[8] One reason Baraka was originally drawn to the white avant-garde was that their inversions seemed similar to those in which blacks were often engaged. But in creating his own black poetry, Baraka has transformed the avant-garde poem, an achievement that should be recognized as an extension of avant-garde art. These transformations begin in Baraka's cultural nationalist poems, with *Black Magic* (1969), and continue through the Marxist poems of the 1970s and 1980s. Through jazzification—the adaptation of jazz techniques and ideas to poetic forms—and avant-garde transformation—the adaptation of avant-garde techniques and ideologies to black poetic forms and historical circumstances—Baraka has almost single-handedly created a new kind of American poem.

One of the avant-garde impulses underlying Baraka's transformations is the desire to "push extreme." In a 1962 letter to the white postmodernist poet Ed Dorn, Baraka confided:

> But I want now so badly to push extreme, and as I see it, the one huge difference between myself and say, Allen G[insberg], i[s] that I have a program (and I don't mean that I am "a Leftist") much more extreme than that name pretends, and certainly less organized, but still a program based on realizable human endeavor.[9]

As this letter implies, Baraka did not find avant-garde political ideas wrong; they simply were not radical enough. Baraka's claim that he was not a leftist meant that in 1962 he did not think of himself as a Marxist. Clearly, however, the "program" to which he refers, his sociopolitical plan to transform society, was one of the factors that drove him to Marxism a little over a decade later. In his letter to Dorn, Baraka notes that he wants something more complex than the terrorism popularly associated with Cuban activist Che Guevara. He concludes: "I want to put together a body of work that will at least provide some text that can at least be referred to in the event of the desired explosion." As Whitman wanted to write a Bible for a new world, so,

8. *The Theory of the Avant-Garde*, p. 56.

9. LeRoi Jones to Edward Dorn, 19 November 1962 (Lilly Library, Indiana University).

in this period, Baraka wanted to provide an instruction manual for the apocalypse. His vision transcended "mere" political change; he was looking for the destruction that will accompany the Final Days. Two years later, in a prose-poem/essay entitled "The Last Days of the American Empire," he indicated the reasons for his extremism when he argued that conventional procedures will not "change the basic structure of the society" (*H*, p. 206). Instead, he claims, there must be a revolution by the young blacks in which they will erupt "like Mt. Vesuvius to crush in hot lava these willful maniacs who call themselves white Americans" (*H*, p. 209). In this essay, the apocalyptic dada revolutionary in Baraka was asking for a transvaluation of values. Baraka's revolution sought not only to destroy the Powers that Be—a common avant-garde goal—but also to commit itself to black people.

Beginning with the poems in *Sabotage* (written between 1961 and 1963, immediately following the poems of *Dead Lecturer*) Baraka started stripping away his ornate style, a style he identified with whiteness. Of the poetry before *Sabotage* Baraka has remarked: "The work a cloud of abstraction and disjointedness, that was just whiteness" (*BMP*, n.p.). For a time the poems after *The Dead Lecturer* were similar in style and less obscure in imagery and meaning; later, when Baraka started seriously emulating jazz techniques, they obtained a new kind of ornateness. The "quiet verse," the imitation white song of the Beat period, was replaced by the loud black chant and scream. Baraka negated whiteness by replacing white avant-garde forms with black jazz forms, for example, replacing the quiet rhythms of the Beat poetry with the more frantic rhythms of bop in the post-Beat poetry (especially the recent poetry). However, in Baraka's poetry the substitution of black forms for white ones works in tandem with its opposite: the adaptation of avant-garde techniques and notions for black ends. That is, Baraka uses avant-garde techniques, such as open-form visual poetry and sound experimentation, as well as jazz forms, to create his new black art.

Baraka began transforming avant-garde poetics into black poetics during the 1960s. His essays are included in Donald M. Allen's *The Poetics of the New American Poetry* (a collection of postmodernist theories, 1973) because they grow out of the ideas of

the American avant-garde, even though their cultural national-
ism attacks it along with the rest of the white world. Two Baraka
essays included in the Allen collection illustrate his "blacken-
ing" of avant-garde ideas. The brilliant and suggestive "Hunting
Is Not Those Heads on the Wall" (1964) is rooted in ideas about
art and criticism of the West previously articulated by the Amer-
ican avant-garde, particularly Charles Olson. However, Olson
criticizes the West from within its own traditions, a limited
viewpoint that ultimately provided no escape for him. Even
when he turned to the Mayan culture, it was as an alienated
white man trying to learn from a foreign civilization. Con-
versely, Baraka's critique of the West is from the outside: as an
American "outsider," an American Negro, he could (and did)
stop identifying with the West and begin identifying with the
third world. This was an act at once real and symbolic: while
both poets lamented the death of the West, Baraka could escape
his "death" by becoming a man of the third world. At the time
he went to Cuba, for instance, Baraka thought of himself as a
lifeless Westerner ("We are an old people already") (*H,* p. 62),
but his trip inspired an identification with the third world that
brought him new life. Of course, Westerners have been "discov-
ering" their identification with colored peoples at least since
Paul Gauguin and D. H. Lawrence made it popular, but when
black Americans find kinship with other black people they bring
with them the sense that they have actually lived in a society
that has treated them as colonial dependents. Baraka's co-option
of Olson's ideas, then, makes his predecessor's romance with
the alien Other into a way for the minority American to achieve
a sense of selfhood independent of his indigenous social
situation.

But "Hunting Is Not" is also rooted in Olson's poetics. As
suggested earlier, the title of the essay itself illustrates Baraka's
absorption of Olson's theory of process in that the act of hunting
(the process) is more important than the object of the hunt (the
heads on the wall). According to Olson, the Greek penchant for
abstractions had severed Western man from the flux, the in-
stant, the concrete world. The Greeks emphasized the noun,
nominalization, over the verb; the frozen thing over the living
moment. Olson's "revolutionary" contribution to Western art
was to try to reverse the direction of Western language. His

successors continued the task: for the Black Mountain poet Robert Creeley, "The process of definition is the intent of the poem" (*N*, p. 408), and Baraka echoes with "Art is identification, and the slowing down for it" (*H*, p. 176). In addition Baraka reflects William Carlos Williams's image of the waterfall in Williams's long poem *Paterson* when he writes, "The most valuable quality in life is the will to existence, the unconnected zoom, which finally becomes in anyone's hands whatever part of it he could collect. Like dipping cups of water from the falls. Which is what the artist does" (*H*, p. 175). Furthermore, Baraka argues, "It is what the God can do that is really important . . . I speak of the *verb process*, the doing, the coming into being, the at-the-time-of" (*H*, p. 174, Baraka's emphasis).

"Hunting Is Not" is in many ways a transitional essay, revealing Baraka emerging from his avant-garde background into his new black identification. Written one year before he moved to Harlem, it marks his awareness of a new source of vitality. Both Olson and Baraka attack "the academic Western mind" (*H*, p. 174), but Baraka, unlike Olson, and quite possibly without being fully conscious of it, built himself an alternative to the sterile West. In "Hunting Is Not" as in other essays, Baraka employs examples of black musicians to show process art in operation. Criticizing imitators of great artists, he claims, "A saxophonist who continues to 'play like' Charlie Parker cannot understand that Charlie Parker wasn't certain that what had happened had to sound like that. But if a man tries to understand *why* Parker sounded like he did, the real value of his music begins to be understood" (p. 176). For Baraka "live music"—music that creates itself as it comes into being, that is, jazz improvisation—and avant-garde art are the only two vital artistic forms, and in "Hunting Is Not" jazz is the only form singled out as great art. Without quite knowing it, he was preparing for the self-creating process that would enable him and the black poets he inspired to bring the avant-garde idea of process into its fullest realization.

By 1965, when he wrote the brief essay "State/Meant," Baraka had shifted from the avant-garde search for alternative forms to the espousal of black art. Certainly "State/Meant" looks like a doctrinaire culture nationalist manifesto for black art: "The Black Artist's role in America is to aid in the destruction of

America as he knows it" (*H*, p. 251), it begins. But even this is rooted in the imagist-objectivist tradition of the *mot juste*. "The Black Artist must draw out of his soul the correct image of the world," Baraka proclaims, echoing Pound's dicta that "poetry should render particulars exactly and not deal in vague generalities."[10] Even Allen Ginsberg recognized Ezra Pound's contribution to Amiri Baraka's cultural nationalism; he has noted, "Imamu Amiri Baraka came a great deal out of Pound with the particularism of his Black revolution."[11] Furthermore, the extreme didacticism of the essay ("The Black Artist must demonstrate sweet life, how it differs from the deathly grip of the White Eyes. The Black Artist must teach the White Eyes their deaths, and teach the black man how to bring these deaths about"; *H*, p. 252) springs from the moral didacticism of Pound, Williams, and Olson. In freeing himself to become a new kind of artist, then, Baraka used the tools his avant-garde predecessors had forged for him.

3.

While Baraka's essays reveal the theoretical aspects of his transformations, his poetry reveals the practical. In the poems, Baraka uses dancing, scatting, "songification," and other oral techniques as major elements in the jazzification of avant-garde poetic forms. In this, he was part of a movement to bring black poetry to the people: in 1968 Larry Neal, the theorist of cultural nationalism, declared that the black artist must emulate popular musical performers like James Brown to reach black audiences.

> What this has all been leading us to say is that the poet must become a performer, the way James Brown is a performer—loud, gaudy, and racy. . . . He must learn to embellish the context in which the work is executed; and, where possible, link the work to all usable aspects of the music. (*BF*, p. 655)

Starting in the 1970s, Baraka followed Neal's mandate: he incorporated elements of popular music, especially jazz, into his poetic technique. In addition, Baraka became a great performer;

10. Qutoed from the editor's "Introduction," in *The Imagist Poem*, ed. William Pratt, p. 22.

11. *Allen Verbatum* (New York: McGraw-Hill, 1975), p. 182.

when he reads his poetry, often accompanied by a live jazz group, he rivals James Brown's performances. Jon Pareles, the *New York Times* music critic, gives us the flavor of a Baraka reading:

> Mr. Baraka stalked the stage, microphone in hand, as he de-claimed, preached and sang a poetic history of African-Americans ["Wise/Why's"]. . . . The poems were incantations, made to be read aloud. They centered on a handful of resonant images that were repeated in different rhythms and tones of voice, as the musicians underlined the meaning or played an ironic counterpoint. . . . At its best, the performance was a . . . collaboration, as when the musicians played wavelike crescen-does while Mr. Baraka described the slaves' sea journey, or when Mr. Baraka let loose with a virtuosic combination of scat-singing and talking drum language.[12]

As Pareles so effectively shows, music as well as musical tech-nique became important to Baraka's performance art.

Orality is important to the process of jazzification in Baraka's art because it challenges the supremacy of the written text, a sacred cow of the Western tradition. Performance art empha-sizes the present event over the written text; like live music, in poetry readings Olson's process becomes quite literally the art object itself. Consequently Baraka has moved from being a "dead" lecturer to being an oral poet, a poet more interested in the sound of his poetry being created than in the look of it fixed upon the page. In fact, he has become the John Coltrane rather than the James Brown of the poetry reading. He comments:

> The poetry since the 60s being much more orally conceived rather than manuscript conceived. The poetry is much more in-tended to be read aloud, and since the mid-sixties that has been what has spurred it on, has shaped its line. . . . To me the [text] is a score. . . . I'm much more interested in the spoken word, and I think that the whole wave of the future is definitely not literary in a sense of books and is tending toward the spoken and the visual. ("HI," p. 27)

Beginning in his cultural nationalist period, Baraka created a black poem formally influenced by black radical forms and the-matically concerned with black history, a form he saw as a

12. *The New York Times*, 3 October 1984, p. C22.

counter to the apolitical nature of white avant-garde poetry. In performance, Baraka actually sings these poems. Like Ginsberg and Jack Kerouac, both of whom sang and chanted onstage, Baraka learned during his Beat years that poetry could be sung. In fact, Baraka was first drawn to Ginsberg's *Howl* because of its jazz sounds. But while the Beats provided Baraka with a model for the sung poem, Baraka takes the poem to thematic and stylistic extremes undreamed of by the Beats. Thematically, Baraka's new poem differs from its predecessors by being both political and collective. Central to his conversion to cultural nationalism was a rejection of the personal lyric—the "I" song, the Beat song—and an espousal of collective black expression. Stylistically, the singing revolutionary black poem replaces the quiet liberal verse of the "Rhythm and Blues" (1964) of Baraka's prerevolutionary poetry. In *Dead Lecturer* (1964) he experimented with the chant and scream, forms that derive from black music; by *It's Nation Time* (1970) he had developed a historical poem designed to be sung rather than read. In this he was influenced by third-world poetry almost as much as by American avant-garde poetry and jazz forms. In particular, Nicolás Guillén, the famous Afro-Cuban revolutionary poet whom Baraka had met on his trip to Cuba in 1960, uses Afro-Cuban speech and music to escape the influence of the Spanish conquerors. Of Guillén, Baraka has written:

> Published in 1930, *Son Motifis* is based on Afro-Cuban dance-song rhythms. Particularly Guillen chose the *son* [song] because it is very clearly the merging of two cultures—the Spanish and the African. Before Guillen, Cuban poetry, like other Latin poetry, tended to identify with the Spanish (conqueror) forms rather than the African (slave) forms. (*DJ*, p. 184)

Like Guillén, in "Afro-American Lyric" and other poems Baraka employs Afro-American speech and music to escape the "conqueror" forms; the merging of the two cultures creates a new, freer one for black Americans. For Baraka, white American poetry, even avant-garde poetry, is written in conqueror forms, and Baraka's addition of slave forms (blues, jazz) creates a new music. With Hughes, Guillén, and Césaire, Baraka has tried to Africanize Western verse by grafting Negro forms onto white ones. In fact, it is probably most useful to study Baraka's work in the dual context of third-world and white avant-garde writers. Like other American artists, Baraka had to reject traditional forms before he could create his new ones. Like Emerson, Whitman, and his avant-garde predecessors, Baraka rejected old languages with old ideas, and called for new black songs for his revolutionary black people.

4.

For Baraka, dance and music are associated with life, vitality, and political action. While the early poetry, the Beat poems, expressed Baraka's "white" conviction that action of any positive type was impossible ("This bizness, of dancing, how / can it suit us? Old men, naked / sterile women"; *P*, p. 44), the cultural nationalist poems express his "black" conviction that action is necessary ("You can dance Nigger I know it / Dance on to freedom"; *INT*, p. 16). Significantly, in his shift from the individualism of Beat negativity to the social consciousness of nationalist optimism, he calls for a collective dance:

Dance up and down the street, turn all
the music up, run through the streets
      with the music, beautiful radios on
Market Street, they are brought here
      especially for you.
. . . .
              We must make our own
World, man, our own world   (*BMP*, p. 225)

Like music, Baraka's poems seek to move the reader/auditor, to make him/her want to dance. For Baraka, dancing is synonymous with political activism; thus, dancing "on to freedom" and into "our own World" means affirming ethnic authenticity and engaging in radical political acts. In Baraka's short story "Screamers," blacks riot into the streets because of the wild music of a jazz musician, and in his *Autobiography* (1984) he compares the Newark rioters to dancers: "The people were like dancers whirling around and through the flames" (*A*, p. 260). Here, Baraka's didactic impulse chose what he saw as a central element in black culture and made it a central metaphor in poetry written to incite radical change. In these poems, dancing is a way to affirm blackness and destroy whiteness in both art and life.

Baraka also blackens the white avant-garde poem with scatting—a jazz singing technique that substitutes nonsense syllables for traditional lyrics—and by creating poems more suited to oral than written presentation. Scatting occurs when singers imitate musical instruments. Baraka uses scatting both to incorporate black rhythms into his poems—to make them familiar—and to break down conceptions of what the elements in a poem should be—to radicalize poetic form. Baraka's scatting began in the poems written during 1965–1966, a time that also saw his move from Greenwich Village to Harlem, his symbolic break with the West. "The Cats Rolling on a Cardboard Box" brings scat sounds into a portrait of black street life, asking if the reader "can . . . understand"

> these
> dribble
>   dee
>   bibble
>   dees
>   these warm street shoobies
>   my soul gets off behind   (*BMP*, p. 144)

Here, scat remains at the level of imitative or suggestive sound, syllables that lyrically evoke his impressions of these crowded new streets. In "It's Nation Time" (1970) scatting becomes rhythmic incitement: calling black people to "come together in unity unify / For nation time / it's nation time,"

> Boom
> Boom
> BOOM
> boom
> Dadadadadadadadadadada
> Boom   (*INT*, p. 22)

Later, scat achieves symbolic status; in "AM/TRAK" the speaker explains,

> The vectors from all sources—slavery, renaissance
>   bop charlie parker,
> nigger absolute super-SANE screams against reality
>   course through him
> AS SOUND!   (*SP*, p. 335)

Scatting both imitates the sound of "Trane" and "monk" and also stands for "this shit" "Life asks" if "you" can "play":

> duh duh-duh duh-duh duh
> duh duh
> duh duh-duh duh-duh duh
> duh duh
> duh duh-duh duh
> duh duh
> duh Duuuuuuuuuhhhhhh   (*SP*, p. 334)

In addition to scatting, Baraka incorporated Olson's instructions in "Projective Verse" on the uses of the typewriter into his attempts to incorporate jazz elements into his poetry. Olson laments:

> What we have suffered from, is manuscript, press, the removal of verse from its producer and its reproducer, the voice, a removal by one, by two removes from its place of origin and its destination. . . . The irony is, from the machine has come one gain not yet sufficiently observed or used, but which leads directly on toward projective verse and its consequences. It is the advantage of the typewriter that, due to its rigidity and its space precisions, it can, for a poet, indicate exactly the breath, pauses, the suspension even of syllables, the juxtapositions even of phrases, which he intends. (*SW*, p. 22)

For Olson, the typewriter was the recorder of the human speaking voice; for Baraka, it is the transcriber of the singing voice. For with scatting, Baraka's new poetry rested on what Geneva Smitherman has called a "songified strategy," the rhythms, the "speech-music . . . which employs repetition for effect, the idea being to mesmerize the audience with the magical sounds of the message." Smitherman's examples of "songification" include the intonations of the Reverend McKenzie of Memphis ("I say Lo-rd Lo-rd Lo-rd, do you hear me, do you hear-ear-ear-me-mee-eeee") and Martin Luther King's "Lord we ain't what we ought to be, and we ain't what we want to be, we ain't what we gonna be, but thank God, we ain't what we was," as well as the speech-music of Aretha Franklin and Flip Wilson.[13] Clearly, this strategy is oral, not written.

13. Geneva Smitherman, *Black Language and Culture: Sounds of Soul*, p. 20.

The problem this strategy poses for a poet seeking to incorporate these rhythms into his work is that he must be able to make his reader "hear" as well as "see" his words. In "Afro-American Lyric," from *Poetry for the Advanced*, Baraka availed himself of visual design to achieve his sound effects:

```
Simple shit uh simple shit
uh simple
shit uh
simple
simple
simple
shit
        society's ugly is the grasping class
        its simple
        shit uh
        see-imm-pull
        see-impull
        Seeeeeeeeeee-immmmmmmmmmm
            pull
    Some See - im - pull
        shit
```
                                              (*SP*, p. 323)

Here, word placement indicates how the poet wants the poem to be read. Olson's notions about breath and the uses of the typewriter underlie Baraka's experiments in speech-music. In fact, word placement, phonetic spelling, and word repetition make Baraka's fairly dry Marxist message rather pleasant to hear. Unfortunately, this early experiment does not convey the same pleasure visually. "Songification" was one of the most difficult techniques for Baraka to master, and possibly one of the hurdles most readers could not jump when encountering his work. "Afro-American Lyric" does not appeal to readers unfamiliar with the speech-music patterns with which the poet was playing. These readers see only the crude language and didacticism it contains because it does not successfully capture the stylistic quality Baraka's "singing" gives it in live performance.

On the other hand, "Afro-American Lyric" does thematically suggest why Marxism attracts Baraka:

```
There is no super nothing which entitles nobody
to opress nobody
see-im
```

```
        pull
        Ugly class
        exploiting class
        owning class
        capitalist class
        bourgeois class
        reactionary class
        no super nothing
        no mystical nobody
        nothing so slick, proper,
        out, xtianish or muslimish
        it upholds or justifies poverty
        aint nothin legitimatizes
        this motherfuckin upside down bullshit system     (SP, p. 323)
```

"Afro-American Lyric" indicates that Baraka sees the Western economic system as "upside down" and that he is drawn to Marxism for the same socio-aesthetic reasons he was drawn to the avant-garde, to dada, to cultural nationalism, and even to jazz—because he sees Marxism as a corrective. For Baraka, Marxism is a political manifestation of the jazz aesthetic process, that rhetorical/political method used to transform the white world.

"Class Struggle in Music," a Marxist poem from *Reggae or Not* (1981) that is designed to be sung, reveals Baraka's symbolic use of black music; here, the music stands for the collective emotions arising from a group experience. Eulogizing "the us emotion / the love emotion" (*RON*, p. 15), he elaborates:

```
        a blues emotion
        a black country nigger emotion
        a steel blue blues city thing
        a factory girder reflection emotion
        an assembly line thing
        a love heat
        in we/us—eye
        a love beat
        in we/us—eye
                eyes
                sees
                Blue us
                blue we's                      (RON, p. 16)
```

In this poem Baraka stresses the collectivity of the emotions in black music and, through his proletarian images, suggests their political implications. On the one hand the imagery in "Class Struggle in Music" is transitional, tending toward traditionally Marxist images of working-class life—imagery common to a proletarian poet like Carl Sandburg. On the other hand, Baraka has not abandoned his old imagery, especially eye puns and visual effects: for instance the "eyes" (perhaps collective sight) are more important than a mere personal "I"; eyes rather than the personal pronoun appear in the poem. Again, Olson is probably the source of the eye metaphor: in "Letter 6" from *The Maximus Poems* he attests, "polis [the ideal city] is eyes."[14]

"Class Struggle in Music" ends with a brilliant example of scat writing, a tour de force that culminates a poem celebrating the vitality of black life and emotion:

> Beat beat beat beat
> boom buppa doompa doom
> boom buppa doompa doom
> boom buppa doompa doom
>   yeh,
>   that and
> Boom buppa doompa doom
> boom buppa doompa doom
> boom buppa doompa doom   (*RON*, p. 16)

Heard, this is a dazzling imitation of jazz music; it is like a brilliant instrumental solo. But, although it is clear that Baraka could successfully capture jazz rhythms on the page, he had not successfully integrated them into the poems; they were still virtuoso performances, not collective black expressions. Moreover, performances reach only the audiences that hear them. Not only the genius of Baraka's voice but also the force of his meaning was lost in the process of transcription.

The sources of this and other sound experiments lie in both black and white avant-garde poetry. Langston Hughes also infused the sound of jazz into his poems, especially the poems of "Montage of a Dream Deferred" (1959):

14. *The Maximus Poems*, p. 26.

What's written down
for white folks
ain't for us a-tall:
"Liberty and Justice—
Huh—For All."
Oop-pop-a-da!
Skee! Daddle-de-do!
Be-bop!
Salt'peanuts!
De-dop![15]

Yet a closer influence on Baraka's interest in sound experiments were white avant-garde writers like Jack Kerouac, who, in *Big Sur* (1962), has Jack Duluoz, his fictional self, experiment with reading the sounds of the sea:

"Raw roo roar"—"Crowsh"—the way waves sound especially at night—The sea not speaking in sentences so much as in short lines: "Which one? . . . the same, ah Boom" . . . Writing down these fantastic inanities actually but yet I felt I had to do it because James Joyce wasn't about to do it now he was dead.[16]

As his comparison of himself with Joyce indicates, Kerouac felt that he, with the moderns, was involved in a great language experiment to expand the sound range of the written text. More systematically, Baraka continued his experiments, imitating the sound of jazz instead of the sea. As early as the black nationalist poetry of *Black Magic* (1969) he was trying to stress the sound of his words:

Freeeeeeeeeeeeeeeeeeeeeee
Freeeeeeeeeeeeeeeeeeeeeee
Freeeeeeeeeeeeeeeeeeeeeee
                    EEE EEE EEE
                    EEE EEE EEE
                    EEE EEE EEE   (p. 189)

But his experiments did not begin to come to fruition until the late 1970s and 1980s.

In 1980 Baraka's long poem "In the Tradition" was published in *The Greenfield Review*. This poem, dedicated to contemporary

15. Hughes, *Selected Poems*, p. 224.
16. *Big Sur*, p. 32.

alto saxophonist Arthur Blythe, is Baraka's most fully realized
and completed "epic" poem—epic in the Poundian sense that it
concerns historical events. Baraka describes it as "a long poem,
a poem about African-American history,"[17] and in it, he most
successfully brings together his white and his black avant-garde
traditions. While the thematic concerns here are black, they are
expressed through an art form that derives not only from black
music but also from both white and black avant-garde technique
and theory. Like jazz, this form is uniquely New World, growing
out of two distinct cultures and becoming something new.

The black tradition Baraka affirms in this poem is more com-
plex than any conception of black culture he had expressed in
the past. It is a tradition of heroes:

> Tradition
> of Douglass
> of David Walker
> Garnett
> Turner
> Tubman   ("ITT," p. 39)

And it is a tradition of villains:

>   the tradition of amos and andy
>   hypnotized selling us out vernons and hooks and other
>   nigger crooks

The poem celebrates the griefs and joys of black people in
America:

>   in the
>   tradition of
>
>   life & dying
>   in the tradition of those klanned & chained
>   & lynched and shocleyed and naacped and ralph bunched
>   ("ITT," p. 41)

But while the poem is nationalist, affirming black people, it is
revolutionary nationalist rather than culturalist. In his Marxist
stage, Baraka has seen cultural nationalism as static, clinging to
a feudal and romantic past, and he has seen revolutionary na-

---

17. D. H. Melhem, "Revolution: The Constancy of Change: An Interview
with Amiri Baraka," p. 92.

tionalism as committed to a struggle for a free and socialist future. According to Baraka, the revolutionary nationalist, like the cultural nationalist, believes like Marx "It is not enough to understand the world; we must change it" (*DJ*, p. 197), but unlike the nationalist the revolutionary knows the world can be changed only by organized revolution, not spontaneous revolt. In the poem Baraka affirms black music—and implicitly, black Americans—as a new form, a new force:

> dont tell me shit about the tradition of slavemasters
> & henry james I know about it up to my asshole in it
> dont tell me shit about bach mozart or even ½nigger
> beethoven
> get out of europe if you can
> cancel on the english depts this is america
> north, this is america
> where's yr american music
> gwashington won the war
> where's yr american culture southern agrarians
>   academic aryans
>   pennwarrens & wilburs
>   say something american if you dare
> if you
>   can
>   where's yr american
>   music
>   Nigger music?   ("ITT," p. 43)

This section of the poem draws on Pound's and Olson's spelling techniques ("yr american"); routine use of lowercase letters, established by avant-garde writers like Cummings; projective verse; composition by field (in which the poet uses the space of the entire page for his "field"); and a demand for American rather than English literature that comes directly from the postmodernists' orthodoxy and attacks on the New Critics. Yet the poem sounds like a black rather than a Beat poem because it is rooted in the specifics of Afro-American culture and is written from that point of view.

Thematically, "In the Tradition" indicates that Baraka's shift from cultural to revolutionary nationalism inspired him to embrace cultures other than the black; for instance, he reveals a sense of kinship with the Irish by arguing that twentieth-century British literature is actually Irish:

> you say nay you mean irish irish literature you mean, for the
> last century you mean, when you scream say nay, you mean
> yeats,
> synge, shaw, wilde, joyce, ocasey, beckett, them is, nay them is
> irish, they's irish, irish, irish as the ira   ("ITT," p. 43)

Although the Irish example is not new for Baraka—he has always thought of the Irish as exemplars of nationalist literature—here he associates nationalism with radical politics (the IRA). In addition, he now celebrates the indigenous music of the southern whites—country and western—because he sees it, too, as the song of an oppressed people. Marxism, then, has given Baraka a broader field from which to project his Manichaean vision; his evaluation of cultural expressions depends on his ability to see them as protests.

As well as borrowing avant-garde techniques, in "In the Tradition" Baraka also drew on the tradition of naming that, in this country, has had its exemplars in Walt Whitman and Allen Ginsberg. While Baraka has always named, he never before so completely used naming as the main poetic device of the poem. As if it is a magic formula, he names the people in *his* tradition to counter those in the *other:* "the tradition of slavemasters" that wants to dominate the world. Baraka addresses the enemy:

> Yet, in a casual gesture, if its talk you want, we can say
> Cesaire, Dumas, Depestre, Romain, Guillen
> You want us to say Dumas, Pushkin, Browning, Beethoven
> You want Shaka, Askia, (& Roland Snellings too)
>   Mandigo, Nzinga, you want us to drop
>   Cleopatra on you or Hannibal
>   what are you masochists
>   paper iron chemistry
>   & smelting
>   I aint even mentioned
>   Toussaint or Dessaline
>   or Robeson or Ngugi
> . . . .
> But just as you rise up to gloat I scream COLTRANE!
>   STEVIE WONDER!

MALCOLM X!
ALBERT AYLER!
THE BLACK ARTS!   ("ITT," pp. 41, 42)

You designates the white man, who is supposed to be dazzled by the names, which evoke the power and creativity of the black tradition. Interestingly, Baraka's Marxist tone is lighter than his black nationalist one: instead of calling "woe on you, white man," as he would have done in the past, here Baraka playfully illustrates black achievement. "In the Tradition" also celebrates and employs black musical techniques:

> tradition of monks & and outside dudes
> of marylous and notes hung vibrating blue just beyond just after
> just before just faster just slowly twilight crazier than
>   europe or its
> racist children
>   be-doo dee doop bee-doo ddoo dopp (arthur
>   tradition   ("ITT," p. 40)

A driving jazz rhythm is created through the repetition of "just," and the scatting of the following lines is more fully integrated than the scatting of earlier work, functioning as a musical comment on the meaning of the foregoing lines. "In the Tradition" illustrates the maturing of Baraka's jazz aesthetic process: by making avant-garde techniques serve black revolutionary goals, Baraka has learned to capture the essence of black oral art on paper. In the process, he has become a successful didactic artist. The poem builds an emotional and historical momentum capable of supporting his concluding declaration that the black tradition is a fighting one and his call for "DEATH TO THE KLAN." The jazz aesthetic process has become the vehicle for communicating a political message through a genuinely poetic form.

> ours is one particular
> one tradition
> of love and suffering truth over lies
> and now we find ourselves in chains
> in the tradition says plainly to us fight plainly to us
> fight, thats in it, clearly, we are not meant to be slaves
> it is a detour we have gone through and about to come out
> in the tradition of gorgeous Africa blackness

says to us fight, its all right, you beautiful
as night, the tradition
thank you langston/arthur
says sing
says fight
in the tradition, always clarifying, always new and centuries old
says
    Sing!
    Fight!
        Sing!
        Fight!
            Sing!
            Fight! &c. &c.
                Booshee dooooo de dooo dee dooo
                dooooooooooo!
                DEATH TO THE KLAN!   ("ITT," pp. 45–46)

Currently, Baraka is composing a long historical poem—perhaps book-length—that examines Afro-American slavery, both actual and spiritual, before and after the American Civil War. He expects it to take several years to complete. The first thirteen sections appear as an appendix to this book, and the earlier sections have been published in a number of places. In this poem, too, formal innovations characteristic of the white avant-garde are transformed through the jazz aesthetic process into vehicles for communicating black revolutionary nationalism. "Wise/Why's" concerns black peoples' need to keep their language because it is crucial to their identity. Language here means not only the African languages lost when Africans were transported to the New World and forbidden to speak their own tongues but also the Afro-American dialects that embody the Afro-American identity.

If you ever find
yourself, some where
lost and surrounded
by enemies
who wont let you
speak in your own language
who destroy your statues
& instruments, who ban
your oom boom ba boom
then you are in trouble

deep trouble
they ban your
oom boom ba boom
you in deep deep
trouble

                                ("Wise 1")

In this poem black music represents articulate black speech—the true expression of the Afro-American nation. Banning the "oom boom ba boom" means banning black culture. Here the scat sounds of "oom boom ba boom" symbolize the identity of black people in America. By substituting scat sounds for readily meaningful words, that is, by using scat sounds as symbols fully integrated into the meaning of the text, Baraka finally demonstrates his mastery of scat. In this poem, scat works both orally and visually on the page. In "Class Struggle in Music" scat was imitative and suggestive; in "In the Tradition" it commented on meaning and helped propel the poem forward; here it is integrated, symbolic, and musically successful. It identifies ethnicity and amplifies the meaning of the poem. It is a major element in the transformation of this avant-garde poem into a black one. In "Wise/Why's" scatting becomes a new language employed to explore the results of losing an old one.

Baraka does more than re-create the language of black people in his poem, however; he also moves beyond black English and standard English to a synthetic language drawing on both:

I was of people
caught in deep trouble
like I scribe you
some deep trouble, where
enemies had took us
surrounded us/in they
country
then banned our
oom boom ba boom

                                ("Wise 2")

Here Baraka exploits the richness of several tongues. In the context of the poem, "scribe" is a fabricated word suggestive of both "describe" and "scribe" (as in "write"); the latter inspires images of ancient civilizations. Together, both associations create a kind of modernist pun. In addition, the substitution of the subjective for the possessive form of the first-person plural

("they country") and the nonstandard past tense ("had took")
are black English; as we have seen, "oom boom ba boom" is
scat. The texturing here is remarkable both in its multileveled
associations and in its larger poetic context—Baraka is unusual
in creating verbal textures during a time of ever flattening sound
in American verse. Finally, the images of black musicians con-
tinue to convey Baraka's notions of heroism: his conscious
model is still John Coltrane, the avant-garde black artist who
attempted to destroy white music so that black music could be
born. Section 4 of "Wise/Why's" concludes:

> in those crazy dreams I called myself
> Coltrane
> bathed in a black and red fire
> in those crazy moments I called myself
> Thelonious
> & this was in the 19th century!

A brief comparison of "Wise/Why's" and "It's Nation Time"
shows the distance Baraka has come in his effort to expand
("push extreme"), invert, and finally fuse white avant-garde
poetic forms with black jazz forms to create a revolutionary
black poetry. In "It's Nation Time" scatting was still experimen-
tal; it remained at the level of "mere" sound. In "Wise/Why's,"
it has been raised to a symbolic level. In addition, "It's Nation
Time" found its lyricism in the cadences of standard English
("reach back to the constant silence / in our lives, where the
ideas line up to be graded, and get a / better one"; p. 9), while
"Wise/Why's" finds lyricism in the cadences of black English
("son / singing, think he bad / cause he / can speak / they
language"). Moreover, "It's Nation Time" dealt only with the
present, lamenting "a people without knowledge of itself"
(p. 7), while "Wise/Why's" reaches back to visions of Africa
("what vision in the blackness / of Queens / of Kings") and sees
a continuity of black language from slave laments ("that sweet
verse / you made") to jazz (the slave narrator's "crazy dreams"
of being John Coltrane and Thelonious Monk.) Finally
"Wise/Why's" fuses standard and black English to create a
speaker who can tell the story of the black man's struggle to
understand the importance of keeping his own identity—his
song—in America:

Son singin
fount some
words/Son
singin
in that other
language
talking bout "bay
bee, why you
leave me
here," talkin bout
"up unner de sun
cotton in my hand."   ("Wise 3")

Amiri Baraka, then, has at once rejected and expanded white avant-garde poetry through a process in which he transforms avant-garde images, techniques, and politics into material that can serve his own visions of black revolution. Rooted in the modernist "tradition," he has fused the exigencies of black history to the methods of white artistic radicalism. Although he seems to reject the modernist influence, in fact he has continued to pursue its goals. Even his attacks on vested American interest groups spring from the tradition of Beat dada. Despite his rejection of his fathers, Baraka may prove to be one of the best avant-garde poets of the second generation.

5. Amiri Baraka's
Significance and Influence ✍

As both theorist and practitioner, Amiri Baraka was the central figure of the 1960s Black Arts Movement. In these roles, he changed both the nature and the form of the post–World War II Afro-American poem, acting as the Ezra Pound, the energetic artist-shaper, of the contemporary black poem. Many black artists and scholars would agree with Haki Madhubuti when he proclaimed Baraka to be "the acknowledged 'Father' of the present day black arts movement."[1] In addition to being a prime influence on other poets, Baraka has also created an original body of work that belongs in the forefront of innovative avant-garde poetry regardless of ethnic background. As a contemporary artist Baraka must be ranked with John Coltrane, Ralph Ellison, Norman Mailer, Charles Olson, and Gary Snyder. His essays alone constitute an original and suggestive body of work. That his own artistic abilities transcend particular political milieus is suggested by the fact that, although the Black Arts Movement has died, Baraka's influence and creativity have not. As of 1985, Baraka has recently published two new books and is at work on a long poem.

1.

The nature of Baraka's poetic achievement is multifaceted, beginning with formal innovations, fusing these to a radical critique of the West, and showing other contemporary poets how to write politically engaged poetry. As Richard Poirier has said of Norman Mailer, "One characteristic of the very ambitious writer is that he becomes a theoretician of his own work.

1. Don L. Lee (Haki Madhubuti), "Introduction," in *Black Spirits,* ed. Woodie King (New York: Vintage, 1972), p. xxvi.

In being so, he manages to set the terms for the criticism sub-sequently written about him."[2] Baraka's ambition differs from Mailer's: Baraka has strived to be a theoretician not only of his own work but for an entire generation of black writers. He has set the terms by which both he and others must be evaluated. Despite his obvious faults—among them, his ten-year assump-tion of an anti-Semitic stance, his absolutism, his Manichaeism, and his penchant not to rewrite—he is a serious artist who has to be taken on his own terms because, like most major modern writers, he makes his own terms.

Not long ago, a white woman in her thirties told me that she had only recently discovered that Amiri Baraka was a poet. An aspiring poet herself, she still had missed this important artist. But the Baraka the white world knows is a very different artist from the one the black world knows. Baraka's fame in the white world comes from one play, *Dutchman*, published in 1964; since then whites have lost track of him. Yet, in addition to more plays, he has also produced a large body of poetry, much of it angry. The majority of the pieces included in *Selected Poems* are written specifically from a black perspective. Before *Dutchman* there were only two books of poetry, *Preface* and *Dead Lecturer*. Only *Preface*, a short book of some fifty-seven pages, is free from ethnic torment, and in both it is apparent that, despite his sym-pathy with the white avant-garde, Baraka was also moving closer and closer to disillusionment with that world. Since Bar-aka's second book, most of which was written in 1961, he has been attempting to carve out a politically committed black art. White readers' ignorance of Baraka's work, then, stems from the confluence of his new direction with their unfamiliarity with the developments of black American art.

The white response to this black art has been either silence or anger—and, in a few cases, sadness. An exception to the general white response has come from the post–World War II avant-garde and its critics, both of which have continued to be inter-ested in Baraka's post-avant-garde developments. But, in the main, the reaction has been indignation or cold silence. Typical of white response have been *New York Times* articles claiming, "Despite all his charges of racism, his glorification of the mysti-

2. *Norman Mailer*, p. 1.

cal supremacy of blackness resembles nothing quite so much as Hitler's celebrations of Aryanism," and "But his early work is far better than his recent efforts: he now seems content to express his Marxism in the most reductive, shrill Propaganda."[3] One general complaint is that Baraka has forsaken art for politics; its underlying assumption, of course, is that art and politics cannot mix. Another common accusation holds that Baraka used to be a good poet before be became a virulent racist. These accusations are not without basis. Much of the poetry in *Black Magic* is hate-filled. The grounds for these hatreds deserve investigation, however—especially as they function to exorcise Baraka's white past—and there are many good poems in a new mode that critics have ignored. It is clear now that the reason the aspiring white poet was not aware of Baraka's poetry was that Baraka had been dismissed by the white cultural establishment and his work was largely invisible for white readers.

The reaction to Baraka in most of the black world has been very different from that in the white. In the black world Baraka is a famous artist. He is regarded as a father by the younger generation of poets; he is quoted in the streets—a fame almost never claimed by an American poet—and he is a force that pushed older poets such as Gwendolyn Brooks to reconsider the nature of their art. Moreover, the black critical response has been enthusiastic. Nikki Giovanni proclaims, "You see it now. The Black Renaissance is born. Joy to the world. LeRoi Jones moved uptown. Wrote plays in the vernacular and a people found our voice." Ntozake Shange comments, "the work as leroi jones does not overshadow the work of imamu technically." Stephen Henderson notes, "[Baraka] is the central figure of the new black poetry awakening." And Addison Gayle says, "The years between 1940 and 1952 may well be called the age of Richard Wright, who dominated the literature and gave it direction. The years from 1965 to the present belong to Imamu Baraka."[4]

3. Christopher Lehmann-Haupt, review of *The Autobiography of LeRoi Jones, The New York Times*, 23 January 1984, p. C22; and Daryl Pinckney, "The Changes of Amiri Baraka," *The New York Times Book Review*, 16 December 1979, p. 9.

4. Nikki Giovanni, *Gemini*, p. 128; Ntozake Shange, *Nappy Edges*, p. 8; Stephen Henderson, *Understanding the New Black Poetry: Black Speech and Black Music as Poetic References*, p. 380; and Addison Gayle, *The Way of the New World: The Black Novel in America*, p. 255.

Clearly, white and black critics are seeing two very different writers.[5]

A large hurdle for white critics has been the criteria they bring to bear on Baraka's work. One of the legacies of the 1960s and the black aesthetic, defined by Houston Baker as "a distinctive code for the creation and evaluation of black art,"[6] is that black writing can no longer be judged by mainstream standards. Baraka's talent is expressed in ethnic terms in much the same way as is John Coltrane's, but this concept seems to present more of a problem in literary than in musical circles. That is, no contemporary music critic would try to evaluate Coltrane by the same criteria by which he or she would evaluate Mozart; it is obvious that they are two radically different artists who must be judged by radically different criteria. Yet, for some reason, literary critics are constantly trying to compare apples and oranges. Reasoning along parallel lines, the white Marxist critic H. Bruce Franklin argues:

> What the academic establishment presents as American literature is still basically the literature of certain white people. . . . I do not mean to suggest that Black literature was excluded from the canon of American literature because of the skin color of its authors. If those professors editing anthologies, surveying the literary history, and teaching the courses, could have found some Blacks who wrote like the white men they admired they would have been only too pleased to include them in their pantheon. These gentlemen are pained and shocked to hear themselves accused of racism, because they are merely applying the same criteria to Black literature as they do to all literature. That is precisely the point, for the criteria they apply are determined by their own nation and class, and Afro-American literature conforms to criteria determined by a different nation and a different class.[7]

5. I want to make it clear that the response to Baraka is not just a simple matter of race—my argument only represents general tendencies. For example, such white critics as Werner Sollors and Kimberly Benston have been very sensitive to Baraka's evolving aesthetics and poetry, and such black critics as J. Saunders Redding and Albert Murray have been very hostile and at times unfair. In the final analysis, race is less important here than ideology and world view. This is not always obvious since race and ideology are often aligned.

6. "Generational Shifts and the Recent Criticism of Afro-American Literature," p. 6.

7. "'A' Is for Afro-American: A Primer on the Study of American Litera-

Central to Franklin's argument is the insight that the single standard is unconsciously racist because it applies criteria only appropriate for one class and nation. In essence, this position is also the main burden of the argument for a black aesthetic. According to the theoreticians of the black aesthetic—and Baraka is one of its foremost architects—the black artist must express his unique experience in America through unique forms; his art, consequently, must be judged by criteria that take those unique forms into consideration. The concern is not just with quality but also with the criteria for determining it; black artists and critics were seeking to develop methods of evaluation that grew out of the culture that produced the art being evaluated.

Franklin's analysis supports not only Baraka's Marxist ideas about culture but also the cultural nationalist theories Baraka had held earlier. In 1963 Baraka noted:

> Words' meanings, but also the rhythm and syntax that frame and propel their concatenation, seek their culture as the final reference for what they are describing of the world. An A flat played twice on the same saxophone by two different men does not have to sound the same. If these men have different ideas of what they want this note to do, the note will not sound the same. Culture is the form, the overall structure of organized thought (as well as emotion and spiritual pretension). There are many cultures. Many ways of organizing thought, or having thought organized. (*H*, p. 170)

This brief quotation suggests the direction of Baraka's ideas. It is not surprising that his thought influenced a great many people; what is surprising is that greater attention has not been paid to it in critical quarters. Certainly his theoretical mind is as good as that of any of the postmodernists, including Olson, Creeley, and Snyder. Baraka's theory is the other side of his cultural nationalism; he was developing standards to use in judging art that springs from particular cultural circumstances. In the final analysis this is the major contribution of the black aesthetic and of much of Baraka's critique of the West—with the other black aestheticians he offers a radical critique of and challenge to the West's evaluative criteria. This critique is of great importance because it dethrones the West's illusion of objective evaluation;

---

ture," pp. 55–56. Quoted by Baraka in his collection *Daggers and Javelins: Essays, 1974–1979*, p. 160.

it challenges the Western humanist, like the scientist before him, to look at his evaluative process and face his own biases. Like the ancient Greeks, who defined "man" and "universal" in purely Greek terms, modern Westerners have developed standards that reflect their own points of view. In contrast, Baraka and the black aestheticians allow black men to see themselves by providing definitions of man and art that do not depend on Western biases.

Since *The Dead Lecturer,* Baraka has been forging a radical political art that should enter him on the lists with other significant American writers of the left, writers such as Langston Hughes, Richard Wright, Kenneth Patchen, and Kenneth Rexroth. Baraka has not only helped rejuvenate political art in America but has also helped expand the postwar idea of the poem. As it was in the thirties, in the hands of Baraka and his heirs the poem is a weapon again; a much more sophisticated weapon because Baraka brings to his black political art the advanced techniques of the modernists and the postmodernists, making him an American Brecht or Godard. In addition to creating an advanced political art with which white critics have yet to come to terms, such provocative and challenging poems as "A Poem for Black Hearts" and "In the Tradition," he has also produced the challenging body of political aesthetic writing to be found in *Home, Raise,* and *Daggers and Javelins.* Though there are other examples of political and social poets—among them Adrienne Rich, Denise Levertov, Robert Lowell, Robert Bly, and Gary Snyder—few American poets embody the revolutionary ethos as Baraka does, and few can equal his poetic theory.[8] Moreover, as a social activist Baraka acts as a conscience for other black poets. On the evening of 23 November 1980, at a forum on black literature in the 1980s, both James Baldwin and Toni Morrison deferred to Baraka as the senior revolutionary; the deference of

8. It could be argued that Adrienne Rich in such works as *On Lies, Secrets, and Silence* (1979) and Gary Snyder in such works as *Earth House Hold* (1969) embody as challenging a political poetics as Baraka. Still, Baraka has produced a larger body of political-theoretical writings, and if we include his two books on music—*Blues People: Negro Music in White America* (1963) and *Black Music* (1968)—with his other aesthetic-theoretical writings, it is hard to think of another contemporary poet who has been so devoted to critical theory. For an excellent discussion of Snyder as a social-political poet, see Charles Molesworth's *Gary Snyder's Vision: Poetry and the Real Work* (Columbia: University of Missouri Press, 1983).

these significant artists indicates the power and esteem Baraka has won among black American artists.

Baraka's satirical bent, in both his work and his speech, is probably one reason his statements so often offend. Even he confesses that "that satirical thing" in him

> has always been present in my work. . . . And I think that's been a kind of characteristic of my view of things, even as a little boy, hearing these various dudes I know in this town [Newark] talk about how I used to be when I was a kid. . . . They were just subjected to the same kind of satire and irony, though, in speech . . . and that's why I always had to learn to run fast, because [laughing] you'd say certain things to people you didn't know would provoke them to such an extent. . . . But that has always been there, a kind of seeing, for instance, negative things in a very ironical and satirical way, and really making them funny, with a bitter kind of humor.[9]

Baraka's "bad mouth" is coupled to social critique because he believes incitement is a requirement of his art and of serious art in general. Like the avant-garde critic Kenneth Rexroth, Baraka uses the metaphor of the boy who cried out that the emporer had no clothes to describe the role of the artist. It is not surprising that Baraka has borrowed this metaphor, since he learned much about literature from Rexroth, the old anarchist poet. Speaking of Henry Miller, Rexroth says:

> Henry Miller tells. Anderson told about the little boy and the Emperor's new clothes. Miller is the little boy himself. He tells about the Emperor, about the pimples on his behind, and the warts on his private parts, and the dirt between his toes. Other writers in the past have done this, of course, and they are the great ones, the real classics. But they have done it within the conventions of literature. They have used the forms of the Great Lie to expose the truth.[10]

Baraka, speaking of the artist in general, echoes:

> For one thing, the denial of reality has been institutionalized in America. . . . And any honest man, especially an artist, must

9. D. H. Melhem, "Revolution: The Constancy of Change: An Interview with Amiri Baraka," p. 92.

10. *Bird in the Bush: Obvious Essays* (New York: New Directions, 1959), p. 157.

suffer for it. The artist . . . is a man who would say not only that the king has no clothes, but proceed from there to note how badly the sovereign is hung. Such a man is, of course, crazy—just as I am, something like Kit Smart or Blake or Rimbaud or Allen Ginsberg. We're all ravers, in one fashion or another. (*H*, p. 183)

Obviously, Baraka is indebted to Rexroth not only for the metaphor of the artist but also for the notion that society is organized so that the populace is never allowed to understand the real state of things.

Baraka's desire to express himself honestly at times leads him to attack violently and unreasonably. During a speech at Rutgers University he attacked the "racism in public institutions such as Rutgers University" (*DJ*, p. 291) and referred to the college as "racist Rutgers, the Rhodesia of the northeastern colleges" (*DJ*, p. 295). One wonders how often this speaker is invited back. But Baraka's attacks, especially his racial ones, must be understood within his very particular context, a context that has been examined throughout the course of this study. On a very basic level, Amiri Baraka is an extremist and a Manichaean; his intrinsic response to any problem is to polarize its particulars, choose a side, and carry his arguments to the extreme. This personal proclivity underlies his political as well as his artistic ideologies and provides the most fruitful way to understand his racism and anti-Semitism as well as his genuinely insightful observations about racial relationships in America. As we have seen, Baraka was attracted to the white avant-garde because—as a middle-class Negro from Newark—he saw the bohemians as the opposite to the bourgeois society he was trying to escape. But Marx's economic doctrine of thesis, antithesis, and synthesis might well be applied to Baraka's mental habits: his bourgeois self was purged through his movement into the bohemian Other, but his equilibrium lasted only long enough for him to assimilate "white" avant-garde ideas. Eventually he divided his world into a new set of polarities and struggled, through his cultural nationalist period, to purge himself of his white/Jewish/Western self. Yet another stage is his socialist internationalism.

Certainly one of the impulses behind Baraka's furious assault on whites during the mid-to-late sixties was his need to dehumanize an Other that was, finally, far too attractive. "Black dada nihilismus, choke my friends," he commands in *The Dead Lec-turer* (*SP*, p. 41). In his next book, *Black Magic Poetry*, he chants: "I don't love you" as he moves uptown (*BMP*, p. 55). Utilizing language invented by the military to ease the dehumanization of its enemies, he also commands "Attention Attention / . . . All greys must be terminated immediately" (*BMP*, p. 135). And he reveals his personal conflict in the confessional poem "For Tom Postell, Black Poet" when he admits,

> You told me, you told me
> a thousand years ago. And the white man thing
> you screamed on me, all true . . .
>   . . . You
> screamed and slobbered on me, to hear you. And I
> didn't. Shacked up with a fat jew girl. Talking about
> Shakespeare, I didn't hear
> you brother . . .   (*BMP*, p. 153)

Later in the same poem he proclaims, "I got the extermination blues, jewboys. I got / the hitler syndrome figured" (*BMP*, p. 154). This may be the most self-revelatory as well as the most repulsive of Baraka's anti-Semitic poems: the "jew girl" (his ex-wife, Hettie Cohen) and the "jews . . . talking through my mouth" (the close friends like Allen Ginsberg from whom he learned avant-garde ideas) must become "things" that he can exorcise through ritualistic chants and violent imagery.

As he moved uptown, Jews came to symbolize three things to Baraka: the economic system that oppressed blacks (a common stereotype), a personal past that had to be exorcised, and a cultural group that had lost itself by becoming assimilated. This latter image is especially telling in that it reveals part of the complex relationship between Negro and Jew in America. Be-cause of their spiritual and physical proximity (both outcasts, both often living in the same neighborhood, both with a history of oppression by the larger white society), Negro and Jew have often been seen as standing in the same relationship to the rest of society, and individuals from both groups have suffered sim-ilar anxieties about acceptance or rejection. And, though the social worlds of Negro and Jew have remained separate, artists and intellectuals have mingled in their common quest for acceptance by white culture. In this Jews have been more successful, moving into the mainstream of American art, literature, music, and criticism. But those still on the outside often see successful Jews as having sacrificed their uniqueness for acceptance. The Jew, then, is for Baraka at once "the white world"—the symbol of white culture—and the outcast who has lost his own selfhood by being assimilated. He is a threat to cultural and personal independence, a figure who must be stripped of any power over the spiritual life of the black.

Certainly image inversion figures into Baraka's exorcisms. As we have seen, Baraka consciously inverts images created by the white media for specific political ends; similarly, he turns images of loved objects into hated ones. It is useful to see his stress on image inversion as a part of his modernist legacy: like Pound, who particularized his frustrations about the international economic system into the image of the Jewish banker, Baraka particularizes his frustrations about the economic situations of blacks into the image of the Jewish merchant and his frustrations about the entrapment of blacks in white cultural systems into the image of the Jewish artist and intellectual. Both Pound and Baraka draw on extant traditions of American anti-Semitism (Pound on the Western strain, Baraka on the black); both milk it for propagandistic ends. The modernist penchant for concrete particulars in poetry—oranges and lemons piled on doorsteps—has given us some of our most disturbing as well as our most beautiful poetry, machine gunners as well as red wheelbarrows.

Voice is also a factor in Baraka's violent outbursts, especially those against Jews. Like Pound, who deliberately used an American vernacular because he saw it as a better vehicle than genteel language for telling what he conceived of as the truth, Baraka adopts a tough, violent voice that permits him to articulate the anger he must muster, first, to purge himself and, second, to incite other blacks to revolution. This latter function is nakedly propagandistic: in his most violent period, Baraka did not scruple to appeal to the crudest impulses among American blacks. Interestingly, however, his anti-Semitic outbursts appear only in published work, not in private letters or other papers.[11] Unlike his hatred of whites, his hatred of Jews seems to have been a stance that he assumed under specific—mostly personal—exigencies and that he dropped as soon as the need for it had passed.

Finally, Baraka's racism should be seen as prelude to his discovery of commonality with the third world. His trip to Cuba in 1960 is crucial because it initiated the broadening of his vision that reached its current culmination in his vision of a transracial internationalist solidarity of oppressed peoples. When Baraka discovered that third-world peoples, too, had difficulties extricating themselves from the mental habits—the cultural assumptions—of the Western powers that had colonized them, he at first thought he had found a truly worldwide view that legitimized his own sense of racial and social polarities. By identifying with the third world rather than with the West, he could simultaneously be reborn into a vital culture and justify his own way of categorizing his world. As he came to understand third-world ideologies, however, he found that antiwhite outbursts were less important than discovering and recovering nonmainstream cultures. With the growth of his internationalism, he has become far more concerned with creating new cultural forms than with destroying old ones.

Not long after his trip to Cuba, Baraka started to think of himself as a third-world poet. His example has helped to radically alter the context in which the contemporary black artist is seen. This context has expanded to include not only black American writers from David Walker to Baraka himself but also such poets as the Cuban Nicolàs Guillén and the Martinican Aimé Césaire. As during the Harlem Renaissance, the black writer of the 1980s is seeking black faces beyond the shores of the United States. During the Harlem Renaissance the primary direction for that search was Africa; today it is the entire black third world. For most of his career, Baraka has emphasized the national and international nature of the black experience. Not abandoning his Americanness, he has nonetheless focused on

11. I was struck by the fact that, unlike Pound's letters, Baraka's correspondence contained no anti-Semitic sentiments. It seems that Baraka's anti-Semitism was a public stance. For insight into Baraka's current thinking on this matter, see his "Confessions of a Former Anti-Semite," pp. 1, 19–23.

the universal nature of the black experience in the neocolonial world: "Afrikan People all over the world / Evolving because of & in spite of ourselves" (*SP,* p. 230).

Among Baraka's faults is his reluctance to rewrite. This failing developed first out of the ethos of the Beat Generation, best characterized by Allen Ginsberg's motto, "First thought best thought" (*PN,* p. 350), and second out of Charles Olson's ideas about process poetry. Baraka's desire to "grab for more . . . more of the zoom trembling in its cage" (*H,* p. 175)—the zoom obtained by spontaneous writing—has marred his art throughout his career: the Beat poetry through ambiguity and the cultural nationalist poetry through poor craftsmanship. Although the Marxist poems are well crafted, the often brilliant *Autobiography* needs better editing; scenes should have been rewritten and extraneous details cut. Baraka's important book of essays, *Daggers and Javelins,* is almost destroyed by its repetitive phrasing; one might question the efficacy of a revolutionary art that stultifies. Spontaneous writing, needed in the 1950s as an outlet for an anal-compulsive society, seems, these days, like a worn-out adolescent mode.

A more serious fault is Baraka's penchant for absolutism and Manichaeism. Professed critical "distress" over Baraka's mercurial nature is really distress over his absolutism—over the certainty with which he believes in each of his metamorphoses. With total certainty he was a Beat, with total certainty he was a black nationalist, with total certainty he is now a third-world Marxist. Repeatedly, he will admit only that the previous stages were wrong, not that the current one might be. His conviction of the correctness of each stage baffles, and at times infuriates, his critics. But, as we have noted, the clue to his certainty lies in his faith in his own ability to find the truth. Unlike typical "true believers," his trust lies not in doctrine but in method and in himself.

Baraka's Manichaeism is as unreconstructed as his faith in his ability to find the truth. Seeing the world in terms of good and evil, of black and white, he admits only a few areas of gray. As with his doctrinal convictions, his Manichaeism changes content but not form: in the Beat days the villains were the squares, in his cultural nationalist period they were the whites, and in his Marxist phase they are the capitalists. Artistically, Baraka's work suffers from his Manichaean vision because art that envisions people as "gray monsters" or "superbillionaire Vampires" not only robs them of their humanity and individuality but also lacks moral complexity. On the other hand, part of Baraka's strength as an artist is his fearless zeal to distinguish between right and wrong. Even though his dualism can be crude, it also has great moral power. Moreover, the inspiration for his moralism has always been his awareness of other people's pain. He once confessed in a letter that the condition of the poor so affected him that "I can't sleep. And I do not believe in all this relative shit. There is a right and a wrong."[12] To be a moral agent in the world one must be able to draw the line between good and evil. Baraka has failed not in drawing that line but in drawing it too stringently.

2.

Baraka's influence on contemporary black literture was pervasive through the late 1960s and much of the 1970s and continues more diffusely today. As the central figure of the new black poetry of the 1960s, he influenced popular poets like Haki Madhubuti and Nikki Giovanni and more poetically ambitious poets like Lorenzo Thomas. His poetic presence can be felt in any anthology of black poetry of the 1960s, in poems like Nikki Giovanni's "The True Import of Present Dialogue," with these chilling lines:

> Nigger
> Can you kill
> Can you kill
> Can a nigger kill
> Can a nigger kill a honkie
> Can a nigger kill the man[13]

Or in Madhubuti's more inventive lines from "a poem to complement other poems":

12. LeRoi Jones to Edward Dorn, [14–21] October 1961 (Lilly Library, Indiana University).

13. *Black Feeling, Black Talk, Black Judgement*, p. 19.

> change. be the realpeople.
>
> change. blackpoems
>
> will change:
>
> know the realenemy. change. know the realenemy. change
>
> yr/enemy change know the real
>
> change know the realenemy change, change, know the
>
> realenemy
>
> . . . .
>
> change change your change change change.
>
> your
>
> mind nigger.[14]

Here Baraka's influence is felt thematically, especially in the poem's insistence that murder is rejuvenating for the murderer and in the vision of the black poet as a warrior; attitudinally, especially in the racial Manichaeism; and formally, especially in the free-verse experimentation.

However, the question of black form can be more complicated than the above poems suggest. Even though Giovanni uses the chant effectively, she has essentially stripped down Baraka's chant and made it more accessible to the "brother on the street"; she has not added anything to black form. But Madhubuti taught Baraka to make his poetry sing; from him Baraka learned the "fast rap,"[15] the form Madhubuti employed in "a poem to complement other poems." The "fast rap" is similar to scat, although "fast rap" is a street form, an immediate one, while scat writing tends to be more abstract, closer to complex musical patterns. In a 1979 poem Baraka says, "If Don Lee [Madhubuti] thinks I am imitating him in this poem, / this is only payback for his imitating me" (*SP*, p. 336). The reciprocal nature of black poetry during this period illustrates the poets' common desire to break out of traditional "white" forms, and Baraka's willingness to learn from others signals his readiness to be part of a new kind of avant-garde. In addition to Madhubuti, Baraka ac-

14. Don L. Lee, *Don't Cry, Scream*, pp. 37–38.

15. The "fast rap" is a form in which the "voice is employed like a musical instrument, with improvisations, rifts and all kinds of playing notes. This rhythmic pattern becomes a kind of acoustical phonetic alphabet . . . repetition [of words is] for effect, the idea being to mesmerize the audience with the magical sounds of the message." Geneva Smitherman, *Black Language and Culture: Sounds of Soul*, p. 20.

knowledges his debt to other, less known but more accomplished poets:

> Poets like Larry Neal and Askia Touré were, in my mind, masters of the new black poetry. Larry coming out of straight-out bebop rhythms, but actually a little newer than bop, a faster-moving syncopation. Askia had the song-like cast to his words, as if the poetry actually was meant to be sung. I heard him once up at the Baby Grand when we first got into Harlem and that singing sound influenced what I was to do with poetry from then on. (*A,* pp. 236–37)

Although Neal and Touré are generally thought of as Baraka's "disciples," clearly he also learned from them how to make his poetry more musical.

During the 1960s Baraka was such a presence that antinationalist writers like Ishmael Reed and Al Young often had to define their art in opposition to him and to the cultural nationalism he represented. When, in *Flight to Canada* (1976), Reed presents two characters discussing the efficacy of words against guns, he is responding to Baraka's dicta that soldier poets can change the world. "Words. What good is words?" asks one of the novel's foils. "Words built the world and words can destroy the world," the hero replies.[16] Baraka's response to Reed was: "Poems are bullshit unless they are / teeth. . . . We want 'poems that kill'" (*BMP,* p. 116). For Baraka—as for his heirs—a poem's effectiveness is measured by how much change it has brought into the world. When, in *Yellow Back Radio Broke-Down* (1969), Reed has Bo Shmo, the neosocial realist, say, "All art must be for the end of liberating the masses. A landscape is only good when it shows the oppressor hanging from a tree,"[17] he is satirizing Baraka's functional revolutionary art, art that Ron Karenga said "must expose the enemy, praise the people and support the revolution."[18] Although Reed's art is the antithesis of Baraka's— Reed defines the novel as "anything it wants to be, a vaudeville show, the six o'clock news, the mumblings of wild men saddled

16. *Flight to Canada,* p. 92.

17. *Yellow Back Radio Broke-Down,* p. 40.

18. Maulana Ron Karenga, "Black Art: Mute Matter Given Force and Function," in *New Black Voices,* ed. Abraham Chapman (New York: New American Library, 1972), pp. 478–79.

by demons"—[19] Baraka's artistic position was so pervasive that Reed had to carve out a counter argument to it in his books.

Unquestionably, Baraka modernized the black poem by fusing it with modernist and postmodernist forms and ideas. The black critic, poet, and publisher Dudley Randall contends:

> The younger poets have a teacher of great talent, and while they think they are rejecting white standards, they are learning from LeRoi Jones, a man versed in German philosophy, conscious of literary traditions (see his preface to *The Moderns*), who uses the structure of Dante's *Divine Comedy* in his *The System of Dante's Hell*, and the punctuation, spelling and line divisions of sophisticated contemporary poets.[20]

The younger generation of black poets did learn advanced techniques from Baraka, but they also learned to invert them, turning them into black militant techniques. It is quite likely that the younger poets were less conscious of the source of the methods and of the inversions than was Baraka; nonetheless, they used them for revolutionary ends. Even the most cursory reading of contemporary black poetry reveals the extent to which it was influenced by projective form and avant-garde visual techniques. For example, Sonia Sanchez:

> Sisters.
>   i saw it to
>   day. with
> My own eyes.
>   i mean like i
>   got on this bus
>   this cracker wuz
>   driving saw him look/
>   sniff a certain
>   smell and
> turn his head in disgust.[21]

The layout and the slash in the Sanchez poem come from Charles Olson via Amiri Baraka. Like a projectivist poet, San-

19. *Yellow Back Radio Broke-Down*, p. 40.

20. A. X. Nicholas, "A Conversation with Dudley Randall," *Black World* 21, no. 2 (December 1971): 30–31.

21. Woodie King, ed., *Black Spirits* (New York: Vintage, 1972), p. 186.

chez allows her verse to encompass the entire page, from left margin to right, instead of cramping it along the left margin. Under Baraka's tutelage, Sanchez learned to use avant-garde notions such as Cummings's small "i" to break meaningless conventions and to highlight the speaker's individuality. This coupling of radical ideas and technique produced an exciting moment in American poetry.

Baraka not only set the tone of the black poem in the 1960s— violent, defiant, and independent—in the 1980s he has become the senior revolutionary voice of the black community. Graying hair notwithstanding, he is as fiery and militant as ever. Even though it is not as easy today to trace Baraka's influence, we can immediately see it in the work of Jayne Cortez, Ntozake Shange, and Lorenzo Thomas as well as its continuance in the work of Sonia Sanchez and Askia Touré. The current generation of writers responds to Baraka as a symbol of the engaged and socially committed third-world artist, referring to him "as a major and as a world poet," to quote Quincy Troupe's introduction of Baraka at a black art poetry reading in April, 1984. Because for a long period at the beginning of his Marxist stage Baraka could not get his books published by major publishers, his continuing importance was glimpsed only at black meetings, where he was treated with great respect. Perhaps it is useful to see Baraka as the new W. E. B. DuBois for the black community, the distinguished, learned, and committed dissenter. Perhaps a measure of his influence is the dedication of a forthcoming issue of the black journal *Steppingstones* to a celebration of his work.

At fifty-one, with over thirty books behind him, Baraka is still an enigma to the American literary establishment, which cannot come to terms with this difficult and brilliant maverick. Possibly the establishment's reluctance to recognize him as it finally recognized the other two great contemporary mavericks, Mailer and Ginsberg, rests on the real—as opposed to the metaphysical—threat he poses. At most, the ramifications of Ginsberg's and Mailer's arts threaten consciousness, while Baraka's art threatens property and the actual structure of society. Or, perhaps, Baraka simply has too big a mouth, too much readiness to say the wrong thing. Whatever the reason for Baraka's exclusion, the American literary scene would be enriched by his more obvious presence: we need him to expand the definition of the American poem and to show us how to demonstrate moral commitment. At the very least, we need him to show us that a major poet does not have to heed the rules the establishment has proclaimed to be "universal."

Appendix 1

An Interview with Amiri Baraka

(Reprinted from *The Greenfield Review* 8, no. 324 [Fall 1980]: 19–31).

This interview took place on 15 April 1980 in Baraka's office at Stony Brook. The central focus of the interview is Baraka's intellectual and artistic development throughout his career, from the Beat past to the Marxist present. Although I have somewhat edited the transcript of the tape, the interview is little changed from the original conversation. My main editing task was to eliminate extraneous words, to condense where necessary, and to straighten out tangled phrases.

WJH: Would you discuss the importance of violence in your art?

AB: Well, I think there are two elements: one, the element of action or acting, doing, that always in my mind, has been contradicted by the traditional intellectual posture of theory, the statement or literature as a passive kind of enterprise rather than trying to see one's ideas implemented in the real world. So on one level, it's simply a focus on action, but on another level it's always seemed to me that the violent action was what was really necessary to achieve things that you know needed to be achieved. At first it was simply a spontaneous understanding that I had, an intuitive understanding, that the violent act was what really was a creative approach to a reactionary and static reality, but later on, when I actually began to get involved with revolutionary struggle, a revolutionary theory, it became very clear that revolution was a violent act, but it was an act which had to be rationally considered. I think that most of my focus on violence per se has been a focus, even intuitively, on revolution.

WJH: Could you address yourself to the importance of the 1950s avant-garde, the Beats, the Black Mountain Poets, the New York School, on you?

AB: Well, coming into New York I was first impressed by Allen
        Ginsberg's *Howl*. It was impressive to me because it was dif-
        ferent from poetry I had read. And I was depressed by a lot
        of the poetry I had read because it was mainly academic po-
        etry, poetry shown to me by academics, and I wanted to be a
        writer, but I didn't really want to write that kind of poetry
        even though it had influenced me. When I saw Allen Gins-
        berg I was gratified that I saw poetry that was stronger, open,
        talked about things I could relate to—there was some kind of
        commonality of interest. It was '57 when I came out of the
        service, the Air Force. I think I saw *Howl* some time in '57
        and that's how I related to it. As far as the Black Mountain
        People, the San Francisco People, the New York School, I
        began to meet those people when I started publishing a mag-
        azine in 1958 called *Yugen*. You know, in the process of doing
        that I met Gil Sorrentino from Brooklyn who knew some of
        the Black Mountain Poets—so I got to know some Black
        Mountain Poets. I met people like Joel Oppenheimer, then
        got turned on to people like Charles Olson, and you know,
        Ginsberg connected me up with people like Philip Whalen,
        Snyder, and Kerouac. Then I met, being in New York, some
        of the New York Poets like Frank O'Hara—I think it was Gins-
        berg who introduced me to Frank O'Hara—O'Hara, Koch,
        Ashbery, the whole New York Poet thing. And the magazine
        I published tried to publish all of those, representative of all
        I liked in all of these groups. The commonality of all these
        groups was a line of departure, a line of demarcation. They
        were not writing academic poetry. They were against aca-
        demic poetry. Although in many cases a new academy has
        been raised around some of them. At the time, the point of
        demarcation was opposition to a kind of academic poetry
        which dominated America.

WJH: You didn't think of them as divided off into schools. You were
        responding to them as facing a common enemy.

AB: Yeah, really. That is what it was, and I think that we began to
        have a deeper perception of these various poets as being in
        groups because they hung around together, related to each
        other, and that was the initial kind of substructure of a pop-
        ular front. In the main it was a popular front against academic
        poetry.

WJH: You met most of these people in New York?

AB: Yeah. I was living in the Village, the Lower East Side.

WJH: An important figure to the period was Antonin Artaud. Do
        you think of Antonin Artaud as important to you?

AB: When I read Artaud I liked his Theatre of Cruelty, his statements, his theories. I thought they were interesting, but when I read them I wanted to use them in a different way than he used them. He seemed to want to commit violence on certain bourgeois intellectualism in a sense, and I wanted to transform that into actual violence on society itself, a society that I thought of as oppressive and racist.

WJH: You think that Artaud's use of violence was just to titillate bourgeois intellectuals?

AB: No, I think in a classic way of twentieth-century French intellectuals, he was making a thrust against a bourgeois sensibility, against bourgeois consciousness, and I think that thrust was implicitly political. But France was the leader of the advanced literary statement, because at the end of the nineteenth century they had the first real socialist revolution. Short lived as it would be, it was the Paris commune that set loose a whole lot of advanced ideas, in France, anti-bourgeois ideas. So the whole modernist movement in the beginning of the twentieth century flocked to Paris, because Paris was identified with newness and modernism and then Bohemianism. Wild stuff. Basically anti-bourgeois consciousness.

WJH: Yes, but what is the distinction between your work and Artaud's?

AB: I was making it more overtly political than Artaud. Artaud was to me the blind thrust against bourgeois sensibility and bourgeois consciousness. I wanted to make it much more overtly political and much more focused.

WJH: Would you like to say something about what people now call the confessional mode? Would you say that the "I" in your poems is more or less Amiri Baraka speaking and it is not a persona? And how much does your sense of the confessional derive from people like Allen Ginsberg and Frank O'Hara?

AB: The only aspect I could say of O'Hara and Ginsberg that I could have possibly appropriated was the kind of openness that I always got from them. Ginsberg's openness was a much more kind of super dramatic . . . in some senses. O'Hara's openness was much more casual and personal. O'Hara's openness and Ginsberg's openness might have influenced me because finally I wanted to write in a way that was direct and in that I could say the things I wanted to say, even about myself, and maybe that did help me to lose any restraints as far as doing it.

WJH: Does the term *confessional* make any sense with your idea of poetry?

AB: Not really. I have heard people use that in relationship with Lowell. He may have found the need to be "confessional" because he very seldom could talk personally about himself in poetry, except in the last poetry. But I think for a lot of young poets the idea of talking personally about oneself never presented a problem. It was just a question of . . . it was something that moved one and one should do it.

WJH: Would you comment on the New Criticism?

AB: The New Criticism I always saw as . . . first I saw it as abstract and then, when I finally understood what it was, I saw it as reactionary, in the sense of trying to remove art from its social context, and treat art as if it existed outside the world in some kind of void . . . is just to me . . . was supportive of McCarthyism. You know that when New Criticism emerged in the fifties and it emerged at a time when the state was attacking the radical and revolutionary intellectuals and trying to remove the kind of legacy of the thirties: upsurge of social consciousness, social protest, and social rebellion by saying that art could not be judged by content in the world or how it related to the world. Then what that did was made it seem that all the people who were writing socially conscious work weren't writing poetry anyway, or anyway were not writing works of any merit. For me, it was a reactionary philosophy.

WJH: And it also seems that the rejection of the New Criticism has to do with its emphasis on persona instead of the personal "I."

AB: As if that were not "they" but some other "I."

WJH: The word *Dada* comes up every once in a while and some of your techniques could be described as surrealist.

AB: I have always valued . . . that as one approach to art . . . to actually create worlds in which strange things happen, but these strange things really relate to the real world. Strange or bizarre or seemingly impossible happenings are simply exaggerated realities. I mean, with me.

WJH: You are saying if you use a surrealist technique you are connecting it to real life?

AB: Right. Really trying to exaggerate reality in such a way that people can understand it better. In a recent play of mind, "The Relationship of the Lone Ranger to the Means of Production," having the Lone Ranger be Uncle Sam with a mask on you know, what I mean—walking around the factory—is really exaggerating reality, making a bizarre circumstance so as to make a point in real life.

WJH: Do you think this is consistent throughout your career, in *Tales*, for example?

AB: There were definitely some surreal elements in some of those things, surreal or fantasy. My early reading was science fiction. So I have never felt constrained by quote "surface" realism.

WJH: So you think of science fiction as an influence on the way you tell a story.

AB: Sure. Science Fiction had to have had an influence on me because for many years that's all I read, when I was young.

WJH: Who did you read?

AB: Bradbury's *The Martian Chronicles*. Heinlein's anthologies. Van Vogt. All those people. I read everybody.

WJH: What is the significance of the term *romantic* to you? It appears in your work a great deal.

AB: Romantic meant to me always really what idealism means in a scientific sense: positing worlds and relating to them based on things going on in your head rather than things as they actually are.

WJH: So romantic is related to fantasy then?

AB: To me, yeah. Now, the sort of classical definition of romantic where one defines life according to passion and passion is the only reality—everything else is a sort of preface to passion or a postlude to passion is linked to my view, but I certainly wasn't able to articulate that view until much later.

WJH: Has existentialism been important to you? Phenomenology? And Zen?

AB: When I first came to New York in 1957, spring '57, I had read Zen Buddhism. There was a friend of mine I corresponded with when I was in the service who turned me on to Zen even in the service like '55, and I had another friend who I knew who went to the New School who studied phenomenology—German and French Existentialism—and I came under the influence of that thinking as well.

WJH: I use the term *vatic* to describe your work. Does that term make any sense to you?

AB: I am sure the vatic stance is found in the work to a certain extent. Probably independent of my will, sometimes in the sense this is going to happen prophecy type—speaking from "on high," so to speak—I think that that sometimes comes from a kind of passion, a sense of feeling something so strongly that it sounds like prophecy in the sense that's why you say it. This is going to happen or this is the way things look and so forth. It always comes off as that.

WJH: You don't mention Whitman very often and it sort of surprises me.

AB: My introduction to Whitman came from Allen Ginsberg and Whitman never really turned me on that much. I read at him but he didn't really inspire me that much . . . except in a purely technical sense of seeing that here's somebody whose doing something different at a particular time which obviously had some influence on a lot of people whose work I did like. But never personally.

WJH: Robert von Hallberg says in a book on Charles Olson that he feels that Olson influenced both you and Ed Dorn toward writing a political poetry.

AB: That could be true. I think he probably did. I know that reading Olson's poetry, which I liked a great deal, and I like the fact that he did take a stance in the real world, that the things he said had to do with some stuff that was happening outside of the poem as well as within the poem. There were a lot of people who tried to talk double talk about what was happening in the poem, whether it had anything to do with anything outside of the poem. He was definitely talking about the world. And I responded to that. But I know a lot of what had moved me to make political statements were things in the real world, including poetry that I read, but obviously the civil rights movement upsurge, the whole struggle in the South, Doctor King, SNCC, the Cuban revolution—all those things had a great deal of influence on me in the late fifties and early sixties.

WJH: Could you talk about the tension which exists in your work between the "liar"—using the poem as a springboard—and the passion for the truth?

AB: Well, it is simply like a lot of times knowing what is true but not being willing to face it either in oneself or in other people or the world and acting like one did not know the truth about certain things, oneself even—saying things which are not true when one knows the truth about relationships with people certainly or things that are happening in the world. At the particular time that that poem came out, it was in the *Dead Lecturer*, that whole struggle was one of schizophrenia, trying to puncture fake social relationships and gain some clarity about what I really felt about things.

WJH: In one poem in *Lecturer* you make reference to "your friends" and I guess "your friends" are the Beats.

AB: Right. Most of the people who lived in the Village and the Lower East Side, who I saw all the time, who I had some commonality with but at the same time felt estranged from since most of them were running around saying that poetry and politics had nothing to do with each other, and I was getting much more political.

WJH: Would you gloss two different poems from the *Dead Lecturer:* "A Poem for Willie Best" and "Crow Jane"?

AB: Let me see, the Willie Best poem is again the whole question of how does one relate realistically to one's environment if one feels estranged from one's environment and especially a black person in a white situation. And especially a person who is growing more and more political, and that politics is showing up his closest friends in a negative light but yet having to relate to those friends. Willie Best presents the black as the minstrel—the black as the bizarre funny person, yet the black as victim, and this black minstrel victim having to come to grips with that—with his victimhood, with his minstrelsy in order to change that. I think one interesting thing in *The Slave* is that I had the army, Walker Vessels' army, wear revolutionary patches with minstrels on them. Grinning minstrels. What that meant to me was that would turn that very symbol which had been a degrading symbol for blacks into something of terror for whites. That grinning Uncle Sambo, with red lips and the white teeth would strike fear in their hearts. The terror groups, bearing these patches, would make revolution. So that's my version. Crow Jane is trying to deal with the question of aesthetics and my own feeling for art.

WJH: What does Crow Jane represent?

AB: The Muse really, the Muse as seen as—the Muse in the traditional sense but then transformed through the blues—like "Crow Jane" is really a blues song but I also got it from Crazy Jane, Yeats, and I thought of Crazy Jane as really the Muse of Western poetry.

WJH: OK. So she is the Western Muse?

AB: The Western Muse. Crazy Jane. Right.

WJH: And Crow Jane?

AB: Crow Jane then is like that Muse transformed by the black experience.

WJH: OK. So she is a positive image.

AB: Yes, she's positive in that she . . . see it's a schizoid thing. See because in some ways it relates to the Crazy Jane-Western aesthetic—the parts of it that are not are the parts I can drag out of it . . . that I think I can use.

WJH: Some readings of the poem make Crow Jane white Western civilization.

AB: That's true. Except when she is Crow Jane she obviously has a black exterior even though the interior is still linked to the Western . . . It's a question of what can you get out of it; is there anything you can save out of that?

WJH: You have her die.

AB: The Western aesthetic dies . . . at least my use for it. That whole book, *The Dead Lecturer,* is really about that: The moving away from the whole Western aesthetic.

WJH: So she is that Muse which is essentially a Western Muse but she has some sort of Afro-American aspect?

AB: She has been used by an Afro-American, i.e., me. And I know she has got to be killed off because there is no further use—I can't get anything else from her. Crow Jane is the white Muse appropriated by the black experience.

WJH: Something that is surprising is there seems to be little influence of black writers on your work.

AB: That is true. I think you won't see the influence on my work until the sixties because before that the majority of my reading was not black writers except my contemporaries in the Village. I was raised up, even though I went to a black college, on the standard fare of Western literature, and I don't think I began to read many black writers until I started reading . . . well, I read *Black Boy* when I was about twelve years old. I used to read Frank Yerby and his sword fighting novels, but I didn't read much black literature until I was an old person by the time of the sixties.

WJH: I remember that your famous review of black literature in *Home* is very negative.

AB: That is based essentially on limited reading of the people I came into contact with. I thought of it as bourgeois. I thought of it as trying to imitate white people, white literature. I have always been more influenced by black music because that was something that was not an academic application for me, but something which was all around me and I always loved, so I always thought more about it. Even now when I write articles about literature I have to write a lot about music because I feel that a great deal.

WJH: Your evaluation of writers like Hughes and Wright has changed and you feel more positively toward them today.

AB: I never felt negative about them. I never mention them. I read *Black Boy* and I loved *Black Boy*. That book I always loved because that book I had read. But my contact with Hughes was always peripheral until I got to the Village and even then I didn't really gain a love for Langston Hughes until the seventies. When I began to read him closely and to read his heavy-weight literature. I loved Richard Wright because of *Black Boy*. I never liked *Native Son*. I read *Uncle Tom's Children* in the last ten years and to me that's a great book.

WJH: It seems that your moving to a longer line in your poetry has to do with a rejection of the white world, of "white music" if you will.

AB: I think it has to do with the poetry since the sixties being much more orally conceived rather than manuscript conceived. The poetry is much more intended to be read aloud, and since the mid-sixties that has been what has spurred it on, has shaped its line.

WJH: Can you talk about this a little more? The latest poetry, some of the Marxist poetry, seems like it's really less poetry than it is a score for you to read. Your readings are incredible and I am wondering are you caring less and less about the text?

AB: It is less important to me. To me it is a score.

WJH: What does this mean? In 200 years when you aren't around, are you going to expect people to be listening to tapes of your work?

AB: Yeah, I hope.

WJH: That is really interesting because it means you are moving away from the idea of the written page.

AB: The page doesn't interest me that much—not as much as the actual spoken word. The contradiction with that is that I should be recording all the time, which I'm not for obvious reasons. I'm much more interested in the spoken word, and I think that the whole wave of the future is definitely not literary in a sense of books and is tending toward the spoken and the visual.

WJH: Now, let me make sure I have this straight. So you think of yourself existing on tape more than the written page?

AB: Well, I think it depends. I think that page will be used by people who want to read it aloud. The question to me of a poet writing in silence for people who will read in silence and put it in a library where the whole thing is conceived in silence and lost forever in silence is about over. And I think it didn't really influence many people. I mean if you conceive of how many people are in the world and how many people ever learned how to read. To me it is a question now of people bringing the poetry out as something to be heard, something to reach people and people who will buy the book and want to buy it in the main because they have heard it. A lot of people buy my books—hear the work, therefore, they want to get it because they heard it. They even read it differently probably because they have heard it. When they read it on the page, even if they are not saying anything, it probably sounds different to them in their heads because they heard it differently.

WJH: At one point you embraced the Black Aesthetic and I guess another word we can use is African Aesthetic, and part of this African Aesthetic is conceiving of the poet as priest. How do you feel about that today, and how truly African was it?

AB: I think the part of it I still uphold is that the poet is in society—the poet's function is as an interpreter of society and as a reflector of society. I certainly cannot uphold priest qua metaphysics. That was one reason I dropped Imamu from my name, because when I went to Africa people would say this is Imamu Baraka and people wanted me to bless them because they thought I was a real priest. But the integration of the poet and artist in society as a functioning member of society with that poetry functioning as something positive in that society, I still uphold that, and I think that was the part of it I upheld most, even in calling it African, because certainly that was the function of the griot or the artist in African society. Furthermore, in the main, it has been the function of the artist in Afro-American society. I think in the main most black writers have been patriots—I mean those that are interesting in the least bit—have been patriots—that means they have been interested in black people's lives getting better, that I have felt in the reading of it. There are some few that write obviously who are not interested in that and who are part of a tradition that tells black people to go fuck themselves even though they are black, but I think that is a minority position.

WJH: Even people like Ishmael Reed who say they deny political engagement I think are very engaged.

AB: They're engaged from the other side. I think Ishmael Reed is very political, but it's just a reactionary politics, and I think if you read his book of essays, *Shrove-Tide in Old New Orleans*, in particular his interview with George Schuyler and that whole statement he says about Malcolm X wasn't a leader, that is intensely political, but it's just backward politics. And I wrote a long essay in *Black Literature Forum*, the latest issue, called "Afro-American Literature and Class Struggle," trying to show how these various traditions in Afro-American literature are always at war with each other.

WJH: Can you talk about your intentions as a Marxist artist?

AB: I think fundamentally my intentions are similar to those I had when I was a Nationalist. That might seem contradictory, but they were similar in the sense I see art as a weapon, and a weapon of revolution. It's just now that I define revolution in Marxist terms. I once defined revolution in Nationalist terms. But I came to my Marxist view as a result of having struggled as a Nationalist and found certain dead ends theoretically and ideologically, as far as Nationalism was concerned and had to reach out for a communist ideology.

WJH: Some people have been concerned about you changing political positions, life styles, so often.

AB: I can see people worrying. I just think they should worry about why they don't. I mean because everything is obviously in change. The only constant that I know is in change. When I came to New York I was a young petit bourgeois intellectual from Newark and the Air Force, and I was involved in that kind of Lower East Side intellectual scene because I thought that is where poets and writers went. I got some information, some experience, was influenced by Malcolm X, became a Nationalist like a whole lot of other people. I certainly wasn't the only person to become nationalized by the sixties. And I think the difference is that because I was involved in some kind of organized political struggle that my activism caused me to continue and that continued activism is what produced my communist views. I saw that Nationalism could not solve the questions that were raised by the day by day struggle. I think that a lot of times when people are moved to commit themselves to certain views by certain events they might stay there forever if they have to wait for some more stuff that other people are doing to change them. But if they are actually engaged in some form of day to day activism themselves they will probably find more reason to change.

WJH: What writers are important to you as a Marxist artist?

AB: A lot of writers really. Langston Hughes, Richard Wright, W. E. B. Du Bois. Those are very important writers. But also people like Léon Damas, Aimé Césaire, and Nicolás Guillén, Neruda, O'Casey; there are also people like Mark Twain and Melville.

WJH: Both you and Bruce Franklin think of Mark Twain and Melville as radical writers.

AB: I think of them as part of a progressive tradition in American literature.

WJH: Would you feel more comfortable with Twain and Melville than you would with Pound now?

AB: Well, yeah. See Pound is a great technician of Anglo-American literature. There is no getting around that. In terms of Pound having learned about poetry in the Western poetic tradition and also having done things to change the very character of the kind of poetry was written in this country. There is no way to get around it. The fact that Pound was a Fascist I think points to the kind of elitist flaw in even those writers, modern writers, that you would say be interested in because of their technical ability. But I teach in my classes, for instance, Langston Hughes came to the idea of writing using the speech of the people if you read "The Artist and the Racial Mountain" based on a commitment and love for the people. Pound comes to it in a purely technical dissociation where he sees nineteenth-century poetry as too rhetorical, too purple, too abstract. In almost a purely technical sense, having studied Chinese poetry, you know, the whole Fenollosa's essay on Chinese ideogram. Then he sees the need, in order for the poetry to be more expressive, for it to get to the solid image. But that obviously is a technical demarcation on one hand—because at the same time he does that, he is moving to Fascism. Langston and a lot of the black writers and oppressed nationality writers came to that conclusion because of their relationship to the people and then the content of their work is more progressive than a Pound because it is not a purely technical decision they reached.

WJH: Pound is involved and interested in history and is trying to change history and that is something different from technical. You can look at *The Cantos* as a desire to find the good guys in history.

AB: I see that as important, too. I see the *Cantos* as a positive form. What I am saying is Pound's reasons for changing poetry were technical kinds of decisions he made in terms of: does this work as an effective poem? As opposed to saying the speech of the people will always be the strongest. Like say Mao-Tse Tung at Yenan Forum says: the speech of the people is always strongest because they are making the most intense kind of relationship with life itself. So it is a whole different kind of thing.

WJH: In your interview with Sollors in his book, *Amiri Baraka/LeRoi Jones,* you said that you were interested in perfecting art technically and that maybe the Marxist art is not perfected yet because it is still evolving. What does technical proficiency mean in relationship with your emphasis on the oral?

AB: Well, it means that you have the ability and capacity to express exactly and precisely what it is you have on your mind with as much force as you can see that it should be expressed with.

WJH: But the expression would be in an oral medium.

AB: Well, yeah, that would be its fullest form. That is when it is in production rather than just on the drawing board.

WJH: Is Brecht important to you?

AB: Yes, very much. I am still reading Brecht. His poetry is very important to me but I have only seen a few of his plays: *Man Is Man, Galileo, The Three Penny Opera,* some of the anti-fascist plays: *Coriolanus.* I haven't seen *Mother Courage* or *The Good Woman of Szechwan.* So I'm still sort of getting into Brecht. But I have a great respect for his theory. I read a lot of his theory. I just bought his *Collected Poetry* and I teach some of his aesthetics. I teach a couple of things: one on socialist realism, his thing on nonobjective art and his "Theatre for Pleasure or Theatre for Instruction."

WJH: Thank you very much.

Appendix 2

Wise/Why's, by Amiri Baraka

Wise/Why's is a long poem in the tradition of the Griots*—but this is about African American (American) History. It is also like Melvin Tolson's *Liberia*, William Carlos Williams's *Paterson*, Charles Olson's *Maximus* in that it tries to tell the history/life like an ongoing-off-coming Tale.

I've been working on the piece now for almost two years, there are already some twenty-five to thirty parts, which are just now beginning to appear.

> *The African Singer-Poet-Historians who carried word from bird, mouth to ear, and who are the root of our own African-American Oral Tradition.*

—Amiri Baraka

Wise 1

If you ever find
yourself, some where
lost and surrounded
by enemies
who wont let you
speak in your own language
who destroy your statues
& instruments, who ban
your omm bomm ba boom
then you are in trouble
deep trouble
they ban your
oom boom ba boom

152

you in deep deep
trouble

humph!

probably take you several hundred years
to get
out!

Wise 2

I was of people
caught in deep trouble
like I scribe you
some deep trouble, where
enemies had took us
surrounded us / in they
country
then banned our
oom boom ba boom

the confusion
the sickness

   /What vision in the blackness
       of Queens
       of Kings
           /What vision
            in the blackness
         that head
         & heart
        of yours

      that sweet verse
      you made, I still hear
      that song, son
      of the son's son's son's
           son
           I still hear that
            song,
           that cry
           cries
           screams
           life exploded

        our world exploding us
        transformed to niggers
What vision
in the blackness
your own hand sold you
"I am not a king or queen," your own hand
if you bee of the royal catch
or the tribes soulwarped by the ghoulishness

I still hear those songs, and cries
of the sons and sons and daughters and daughters
I still bear that weeping in my heart
that bleeding in my memory

And I am not a king
nor trader in flesh
I was
of the sufferers
I am among those
to be avenged!

Wise 3

Son singin
fount some
words/Son
singin
in that other
language
talkin bout "bay
bee, why you
leave me
here," talking bout
"up unner de sun
cotton in my hand." Son
singing, think he bad
cause he
can speak
they language, talkin bout
"dark was the night
  the ocean deep
  white eyes cut through me
  made me weep."

Son singin
fount some words. Think
he bad. Speak
they
language.

'sawright
I say
'sawright
wit me
look like
yeh, we gon be here
a taste

Wise 4

No coat has I got
nor extra chop
no soft bed or favor
no connection w/ the slaver

dark was the night
our eyes had not met
I fastened my life to me
and tried to find my way

talk did I hear
of fires and burning
and death to the gods

on the dirt where I slept
such talk
warmed me

such talk
lit my way

I has never got nothing but hard times and punishment
Any joy I had I made myself, and the dark woman
who took my hand and led me to myself

I has never got nothing
but a head full of blood
my scar, my missing teeth,

I has never got nothing but
killer frustration/ yes dark
was the night
cold was the ground

I has never got nothing, and talk
of rebellion
warmed me

Song to me, was the darkness
in which I could stand
my profile melted into the black air
red from the flame of the burning big house

in those crazy dreams I called myself
Coltrane
bathed in a black and red fire
in those crazy moments I called myself
Thelonious
& this was in the 19th century!

Wise 5

I overheard the other night
standing by the window
of the big house

a nigra say, through an alabaster
mask, "the first negro
was a white man."

Slanty red darts angulate the darkness
my hands got cold, my head was sweaty

like a mystery
story
like a gospel
hymn
like the tales
of the
wizards
and the life
of the gods

I did not know
who my father
was

I only barely
knew
my mother

But I knew something that night
about a negro
something even
the tv cant wash
away

I fount out something
about the negro

the wind may blow
the train dont come
the mayor might belch
his mistress might gain weight

But I fount out something that night
about the negro
& the world
got clear

you can hurray all you want to
you can kiss an elephants ass

But I fount out something
that night, before I slid
back to the field hands quarters
I fount out somthing
about
the magic
of slavery

& I vowed not to be
a slave
no more

Wise 6

Has we come far?

We has come far.

How we got there

How we got where?

Who we talkin bout?

What they name?

Oh, the slave peepas
you the slave peepas

Who the slave peepas
Just the same.

Struggle in dark, come down
the road. Knew your life
your sorrow. Knew your singing
in the dark. Knew the whip

that scarred you. And the century
change, alright, alright, the
years go by in light in darkness

there's white peepa voice behind my air
claim I should be free. They peepas hang out
in the north somewhere, dont need no bread
from the big house man. They voice hang
in the air.

But thas alright, alright wit me.
I preciate all of that.

Thas alright, alright wit me
But I been gone, naw, I been gone

my shape look like black on black
and fading

Wise 7

Back in the forest

the maroons laid

outraged by slavery, & split

from it, when the bombs burst

across the air, and fire tore

mens hearts, they knew some new

joint change was upon the time

and so emerged, a gun in one hand,

something funky, in the other.

Wise 8

From the country
to the city, we left
where things
were pretty—to get away from
the klansmen, and race freaks who
hung with the Slavemasters' cause
who could not believe in democracy
who would not let life be beautiful
who howled moon shadows screaming
for the primitive. Who climbed the trees
for past centuries, hollering for caves
and blood. From the country, to the city
we left where things were
pretty. Got city life, got city bred
wanted rights and services (get to that,
we thought) when all the time
it coulda been better, when all the time
new cdda been, built cadda been, progress
cdda been, and all the great notes of peace
all the great notes of peace
  all that
     cdda
        been

Wise 9

our war
was for
liberation
to end
slave times

now war
is over
we free
they say

who they
who say
what free
gone be?

there are cities
we can go to

there are cities
of light and newing

So what these faces laws hover
these swine wind law death people
these death time rebs return to crow
these slavemaster corpse leap off the flo
these sheet face coward monster haints
these death word carriers and slave lovers

there was war
before
be war
again
died before
will die again
but not gone die
not gone leave
not gone cry too long
not gone grieve
free is who we are and be
love who what will lift us we
struggle love struggle—against primitive death
while you walking round
spirit death tie you down
slave death and servant death and let me work for us to be

Wise 10

So in 1877 the lie grew
we all knew
the heart dead
the lie instead

They talked blood
They put on hoods
They paid for murder
They closed the books

No democracy
No light
primitive times
returned

across the road
the horse men prowled
American guns for African American lives

You'll never vote
you'll never grow
you'll never never never
be free   never
be free

           never

be free

           never
           never
           never

                              Enter Booker T.

Rough Hand Dreamers (Wise 11)

You was a country folk, on the
land. Farmers before farmers
founders of cities, ile ife,*
where the world began. Was creator
of university, I trumpet timbuctoo
because I cannot bear to think
you think Banneker was wilder
than the breed. It was the woman
conceived of familiar cows and
architecture. Yon drummers know
how they are hide curers & musicians.
Now they enter the cities to enter future
reality. Now death, now blood, now hooded

*ile ife—ancient holy Yoruba city

criminals, resistance in its human dimension
like electric theories, post all abrahams.

What was it we wanted = Ourselves!
And why? We had been inside others being alive
for nothing
and worked to death
    our murders
    were circuses
    our murderers
    something like
    clowns

A farmer come to the city (Wise 12)

dirt growing in his mind
songs black land come in to
curl your poetry blind.
Banjo
waves and sinking bones
play eyes on sky
blood music

heaven people
say see heaven
they seeing
up side down

now they say we fought for evil
took our guns, the wise ones hid, say you
never was to be here
you never was to be

kept to edge of city
alleys behind the bossman's
house. got a job, you got a space,
you got a bond to heal your face

changed from slave
to convict, gone
from lazy to vagrant
jail lost boy in sleep
jail house/plantation moan
jail, was how they changed it

we
vote among roaches

Wise 13

And now you know
how "ghettoes"
grow

                                        (you knew
                                        (how ghettoes)
                                         grew?   )

                    (Reality
                           for "you"
                    is minstrelsy.)

Selected Bibliography

Works by Amiri Baraka

Collected Works

The Autobiography of LeRoi Jones/Amiri Baraka. New York: Freundlich Books, 1974.

Editor. *Black Fire.* New York: William Morrow, 1968.

Black Magic: Collected Poetry, 1961–1967. Indianapolis: The Bobbs-Merrill Co., 1969.

Black Music. New York: William Morrow, 1968.

Blues People: Negro Music in White America. New York: William Morrow, 1963.

"Confessions of a Former Anti-Semite." *The Village Voice,* 17–23 December 1980, pp. 1, 19–23.

Editor. *Confirmations.* New York: William Morrow, 1983.

Daggers and Javelins: Essays, 1974–1979. New York: William Morrow, 1984.

The Dead Lecturer. New York: Grove Press, 1964.

Dutchman and the Slave. New York: William Morrow, 1964.

Four Black Revolutionary Plays. Indianapolis: The Bobbs-Merrill Co., 1969.

Hard Facts. Newark: Peoples War, 1975.

Home: Social Essays. New York: William Morrow, 1966.

With Fundi (Billy Abernathy). *In Our Terribleness (Some elements and meaning in black style).* Indianapolis: The Bobbs-Merrill Co., 1970.

It's Nation Time. Chicago: Third World Press, 1970.

Jello. Chicago: Third World Press, 1970.

Editor. *The Moderns.* New York: Corinth Books, 1963.

The Motion of History and Other Plays. New York: William Morrow, 1978.

Preface to a Twenty Volume Suicide Note . . . . New York: Totem Press, 1961.

Raise Race Rays Raze: Essays Since 1965. New York: Random House, 1971.

Reggae or Not! Bowling Green, N.Y.: Contact II Publications, 1981.
Selected Plays and Prose of Amiri Baraka/LeRoi Jones. New York, 1979.
Selected Poetry of Amiri Baraka/LeRoi Jones. New York, 1979.
The Sidney Poet Heroical. New York: I. Reed Books, 1979.
Slave Ship: A Historical Pageant. Newark: Jihad Productions, 1965.
Spirit Reach. Newark: Jihad Productions, 1972.
The System of Dante's Hell. New York: Grove Press, 1965.
Tales. New York: Grove Press, 1967.
"Toward Ideological Clarity." *Black World,* November 1974, pp. 24–33, 84–95.
"Uncollected Works," compiled by Werner Sollors. An unpublished collection of Amiri Baraka's fugitive works, housed at the Beinecke Library, Yale University.
"Why I Changed My Ideology: Black Nationalism and Socialist Revolution." *Black World,* July 1975, pp. 30–42.

Uncollected Poetry (arranged chronologically)

"Slice of Life." *Yugen,* no. 1 (March 1958): 16.
"Lines to Garcia Lorca." *Yugen,* no. 1 (March 1958): 17–18.
"Love Poem." *Birth,* no. 1 (Autumn 1958): 52.
"Scenario." *Naked Ear,* no. 11 (1958): 7–8.
"The Gift of the Unicorn." *Epos* 10, no. 2 (Winter 1958): 7.
"Central Park in Winter." *Quicksilver* 11, no. 4 (Winter 1958): p. 14.
"The Last Roundup." *Hearse,* no. 5 (1958): 16.
"Oedipus Poem." *Odyssey* 1, no. 4 (1959): 56.
"April 13 (for Tom)." *Penny Poems* 30 (1959).
"Parthenos." *Yugen,* no. 4 (1959): 23–26.
"Consider This." In *A New Folder,* ed. by Daisy Aldan, pp. 31–32. New York: Folder Editions, 1959.
"For You." *Jan 1st 1959: Fidel Castro.* New York: Totem Press, 1959, p. 4.
"March." *Combustion,* no. 10 (May 1959), pp. 7–8.
"Spring & Soforth." *Penny Poems* 111 (1960).
"Epistrophe (for Yodo)." Edited by Elias Wilentz. *The Beat Scene.* New York: Corinth Books, 1960, p. 56.
"In JW's Rug." *Provincetown Review,* no. 3 (1960): 69.
"A Paramount Picture (for Nick Charles)." *Neon Obit,* no. 5 (1960): 2.
"Node." *Yugen,* no. 6 (1960): 38.
"The A, B, C's (for Charles)." *Yugen,* no. 6 (1960): 39–40.
"Confucius Say." *Combustion,* no. 13 (May 1960): 3.
"The Disguise." *Penny Poems* 155 (1961).
"Sundance." *Trobar,* no. 2 (1961): 27–28.
"Axel's Castle." *Whetstone* 4, no. 2 (1961): 81.
"The Parade . . . five themes for Robert Thompson: the southpaw; bo

peep; 'x'; boswell; dr. jive." *Outsider* 1 (1961): 67–68.

"Love Poem." In *Junge amerikanische Lyrik*, ed. by Gregory Corso and Walter Höllerer, p. 156. Munich: Hanser, 1961.

"Note from the Underground." In *Junge amerikanische Lyrik*, ed. by Gregory Corso and Walter Höllerer, pp. 158–60. Munich: Hanser, 1961.

"A Long Poem for Myself." *Locus-Solus* 3–4 (Winter 1962): 13–14.

"A Poem for Myself, The Fool." *Locus-Solus* 3–4 (Winter 1962): 19.

"To a 25-Year-Old King." *Nomad/New York*, nos. 10–11 (Autumn 1962): 23–24.

"Riding and Shooting." *Nomad/New York*, nos. 10–11 (Autumn 1962): 23–24.

"The Pimp." *Outburst*, no. 2 (1963): 17.

"Charlie Parker: The Human Condition." In *Soon One Morning: New Writing by American Negroes, 1940–1962*, edited by Herbert Hill, pp. 609–10. New York: Knopf, 1963.

"In Wyoming Territory: In Wyoming Territory (a title); In Wyoming Territory (a veil); In Wyoming Territory (a story); In Wyoming Territory (Music of); in Wyoming Territory (Dance/Like/)." *The Floating Bear* 28 (1963): 5–9.

"Exaugural Address (for Jacqueline Bouvier Kennedy, who has had to eat too much shit)." *Kulchur* 3, no. 12 (Winter 1963): inserted between 86 and 87.

"Engines." *Imago*, no. 1 (February 1964): 6–8.

"DoubleFeel." *Fuck You: A Magazine of the Arts* 6, no. 5 (April 1964): 35.

"Archie and Them Other Cats." *Liberator* 4, no. 9 (September 1964): 16.

"Nana: 1888–1963." *Red Clay Reader*, no. 1 (1964): 51.

"Sunspots." *Red Clay Reader*, no. 1 (1964): 51.

"Like Rousseau." *Poetry* 105, no. 3 (December 1964): 161.

"Target Study." *Niagara Frontier Review*, no. 2 (Spring-Summer 1965): 54–56.

"Chapter." *Niagara Frontier Review*, no. 2 (Spring-Summer 1965): 57–58.

"The Heavy." *Niagara Frontier Review*, no. 2 (Spring-Summer 1965): 59.

"Relurk." *Niagara Frontier Review*, no. 2 (Spring-Summer 1965): 60–61.

"Lefty." *Niagara Frontier Review*, no. 2 (Spring-Summer 1965): 62–63.

"Brides of the Captured." *Niagara Frontier Review*, no. 2 (Spring-Summer 1965): 65–66.

"The Scholar." *Black Orpheus*, no. 17 (June 1965): 49.

"Theory." *Spero* 1, no. 1 (1965): 24.

"The Occident." *Black Dialogue* 2, no. 5 (Autumn 1966): 27.

"Indians." *Black Dialogue* 2, no. 5 (Autumn 1966): 28.

"A Traffic of Love." *Floating Bear,* no. 35 (1968): 16.

"Old Men's Feet (For Dr. Koch)." *Floating Bear,* no. 35 (1968): 17.

"Nick Charles Meets the Wolf-Man." *Floating Bear,* no. 35 (1968): 18–19.

"West of Dodge." *Floating Bear,* no. 35 (1968): 20.

"Spacepoem for Four Tones." *Black News* 1, no. 4 (1969).

"Black Power Chant." *Black Theatre,* no. 4 (April 1970): 35.

"Move." In *Black Spirits: A Festival of New Black Poets in America,* edited by Woodie King, pp. 24–26. New York: Vintage, 1972.

"We Know Directions." *Black World* 22, no. 7 (May 1973): 40.

"OK Shoot!" *Black World* 22, no. 7 (May 1973): 40.

"US." *Black World* 22, no. 7 (May 1973): 41–42.

"In the Midst of Chaos." *Black World* 22, no. 7 (May 1973): 42.

"Look Inside." *Black World* 22, no. 7 (May 1973): 43.

"Habari Gani." *Black World* 22, no. 7 (May 1973): 43–44.

"Postcard." *Montemora* 3 (Spring 1977): 130–31.

"Jungle Poem." *Inc. #1* (1979): 35–41.

"Countries Want Independence, Nations Want Liberation, and the People Want Revolution!" *Unity* 5–18 October 1979, p. 13.

"The Ballgame." *Forward* 3 (January 1980): 145–50.

"The Device." *Lumen/Avenue A* 2 (Winter-Spring 1980): 31.

"Important Sonnet." *Lumen/Avenue A* 2 (Winter-Spring 1980): 32.

"The Last Revolutionary for Abbie Hoffman." *The Village Voice,* 15 October 1980, p. 18.

"JAIL-O!" *The Greenfield Review* 8, nos. 3–4 (Fall 1980): 32–34.

"The Mechanic Sits for a Portrait." *The Greenfield Review* 8, nos. 3–4 (Fall 1980): 35–37.

["In the Tradition"] "Not a White Shadow." *The Greenfield Review* 8, nos. 3–4 (Fall 1980): 38–46. In 1982 Baraka privately printed a pamphlet version of "In the Tradition."

"Sounding." *Black American Literature Forum* 16, no. 3 (Fall 1982): 103–105.

"Poem for the U.S. Bourgeoisie and Their Running Dogs!" *The Black Nation* 2 (Fall-Winter 1982): 19–20.

"Wailers/ (for Larry Neal and Bob Marley)." *The Black Nation* 2 (Fall-Winter 1982): 21.

"Linguistics." *Steppingstones* 1, no. 1 (Summer 1982): 5.

"In World War III Even Your Muse Will Get Killed!" *Steppingstones* 1, no. 1 (Summer 1982): 6.

"Terry & the Pirates' Replacement." *Steppingstones* 1, no. 1 (Summer 1982): 7.

"Bad News (for Charlie Richardson)." *Steppingstones* 1, no. 1 (Summer 1982): 8.

"Whys/Wise" (first four poems). *Campus Exchange Forum* 1, no. 1 (December 1983): no pagination. CEF is a publication of the Black Faculty and Staff Association at SUNY, Stony Brook.

"Wise/Why's." (1–4). *Unity*, 16 December 1983–19 January 1984, p. 14.

"Reflections (Monk)." *Red Bass* (Winter 1983): 20.

"I Investigate the Sun." *Long Shot* (Spring 1983): 16.

"Zoodoo." *Long Shot* (Spring 1983): 17.

"If." *Long Shot* (Spring 1983): 19.

"The Morning After." *Long Shot* (Spring 1983): 20.

"1984." *Campus Exchange Forum* 2, nos. 4–5 (October & December 1984): 3–4.

"Real Song Is a Dangerous Number!" *The Village Voice* 26 February 1985, p. 28.

Works by Other Authors

Allen, Donald, ed. *New American Poetry, 1945–1960*. New York: Grove Press, 1960.

Allen, Donald, ed. *New American Story*. New York: Grove Press, 1965.

———. *The Poetics of the New American Poetry*. New York: Grove Press, 1973.

———. *The Postmoderns: The New American Poetry*. Rev. ed. New York: Grove Press, 1982.

Altieri, Charles. *Enlarging the Temple*. Lewisburg: Bucknell University Press, 1979.

Baker, Houston A. "Generational Shifts and the Recent Criticism of Afro-American Literature." *Black American Literature Forum* 15, no. 1 (Spring 1981): 3–21.

———. " 'These Are Songs if You Have the/Music': An Essay on Imamu Baraka." *Minority Voices* 1, no. 1 (Spring 1977): 1–18.

Barrett, William. *Irrational Man*. New York: Anchor Books, 1962.

Benston, Kimberly W. *Baraka: The Renegade and the Mask*. New Haven: Yale University Press, 1976.

———. *Imamu Amiri Baraka (LeRoi Jones): A Collection of Critical Essays*. Englewood Cliffs, N. J.: Prentice-Hall, 1978.

———. "Late Coltrane: A Re-membering of Orpheus." In *Chant of Saints*, edited by Michael S. Harper, pp. 413–24. Urbana: University of Illinois Press, 1979.

Bigsby, C. W. E. *Dada and Surrealism*. New York: Methuen, 1972.

Bloom, Harold. *The Anxiety of Influence*. New York: Oxford University Press, 1973.

Bogle, Donald. *Toms, Coons, Mulattoes, Mammies, and Bucks*. New York: Bantam Books, 1974.

Boundary 2 (including a supplement on Amiri Baraka) 6, no. 2 (Winter

1978): 303–442.

Breton, André. *Manifestoes of Surrealism*. Ann Arbor: University of Michigan Press, 1972.

Brown, Lloyd W. *Amiri Baraka*. Boston: Twayne Publishers, 1980.

Bruner, Richard W., "Interview with Amiri Baraka," 1970. Schomberg Center of Oral History.

Caws, Mary Ann. *The Poetry of Dada and Surrealism: Aragon, Breton, Tzara, Eluard, and Desnos*. Princeton, N. J.: Princeton University Press, 1970.

Clark, Thomas. "Allen Ginsberg." In *Writers at Work: The Paris Review Interviews*, Third Series, edited by George Plimpton. New York: Viking Press, 1967.

Cullen, Countee. *Color*. New York: Harper, 1925.

Dace, Letitia. *LeRoi Jones (Imamu Amiri Baraka): A Checklist of Works by and about Him*. London: Nether Press, 1971.

Eliot, T. S. *On Poetry and Poets*. New York: The Noonday Press, 1961.

_____. *Selected Essays*. New York: Harcourt, Brace & World, 1964.

Ellison, Ralph. "A Coupla Scalped Indians." *New World Writings #9* (1956): 225–36.

_____. *Invisible Man*. New York: Vintage Books, 1972.

_____. *Shadow and Act*. New York: New American Library, 1966.

Fanon, Frantz. *The Wretched of the Earth*. New York: Grove Press, 1966.

Ferlinghetti, Lawrence. *Who Are We Now?* New York: New Directions, 1976.

Fischer, William C. "Amiri Baraka." In *American Writers* (supplement 2, part 1), edited by A. Walton Litz, pp. 29–63. New York: Charles Scribner's Sons, 1981.

Franklin, H. Bruce. " 'A' Is for Afro-American: A Primer on the Study of American Literature." *The Minnesota Review*, no. 5 (Fall 1975): 53–64.

Gates, Henry Louis. "The 'Blackness of Blackness': A Critique of the Sign and the Signifying Monkey." *Critical Inquiry* 9, no. 4 (June 1983): 685–723.

Gayle, Addison. *The Way of the New World: The Black Novel in America*. New York: Anchor/Doubleday, 1975.

Ginsberg, Allen. *Ankor-Wat*. London: Fulcrum Press, 1968.

_____. *Howl and Other Poems*. San Francisco: City Lights Books, 1959.

_____. *Planet News*. San Francisco: City Lights Books, 1968.

Giovanni, Nikki. *Black Feeling, Black Talk, Black Judgement*. New York: William Morrow, 1970.

_____. *Gemini*. Indianapolis: The Bobbs-Merrill Co., 1971.

Harris, William J. "An Interview with Amiri Baraka." *The Greenfield Review* 8, no. 324 (Fall 1980): 19–31.

_____. "Manuals for Black Militants." *The Antioch Review* 27, no. 2 (Fall 1967): 408–16.

Henderson, Stephen. *Understanding the New Black Poetry: Black Speech and Black Music as Poetic References.* New York: William Morrow, 1973.

Hill, Herbert, ed. *Anger, and Beyond: The Negro Writer in the United States.* New York: Harper and Row, 1966.

Hudson, Theodore R. *From LeRoi Jones to Amiri Baraka: The Literary Works.* Durham, N. C.: Duke University Press, 1973.

Hughes, Langston. *Selected Poems.* New York: Alfred A. Knopf, 1973.

―――. *The Weary Blues.* New York: Alfred A. Knopf, 1926.

Kerouac, Jack. *Big Sur.* New York: McGraw-Hill, 1981.

King, Woodie, ed. *Black Spirits: A Festival of New Black Poets in America.* New York: Vintage Books, 1972.

Kofsky, Frank. *Black Nationalism and the Revolution in Music.* New York: Pathfinder Press, 1970.

Lacey, Henry C. *To Raise, Destroy, and Create: The Poetry, Drama, and Fiction of Imamu Amiri Baraka (LeRoi Jones).* Troy, New York: The Whitston Publishing Co., 1981.

Lee, Don L. *Don't Cry, Scream.* Detroit, Mich.: Broadside Press, 1970.

Levertov, Denise. *The Poet in the World.* New York: New Directions, 1973.

Mackey, Nathaniel. "The Changing Same: Black Music in the Poetry of Amiri Baraka." *Boundary 2* 6, no. 2 (Winter 1978): 355–86.

Melhem, D. H. "Revolution: The Constancy of Change: An Interview with Amiri Baraka." *Black American Literature Forum* 16, no. 3 (Fall 1982): 87–103.

Mersmann, James F. *Out of the Vietnam Vortex: A Study of Poets and Poetry Against the War.* Lawrence: University Press of Kansas, 1974.

O'Hara, Frank. *The Selected Poems.* New York: Vintage Books, 1974.

Olson, Charles. *The Maximus Poems.* New York: Jargon/Corinth Books, 1960.

―――. *Selected Writings.* New York: New Directions, 1966.

―――. *The Special View of History.* Berkeley: Oyez, 1970.

O'Meally, Robert G. *The Craft of Ralph Ellison.* Cambridge: Harvard University Press, 1980.

Ossman, David, ed. *The Sullen Art.* New York: Corinth Books, 1963.

Parkinson, Thomas, ed. *A Casebook on the Beat.* New York: Thomas Y. Crowell, 1961.

Paz, Octavio. *Children of the Mire: Modern Poetry from Romanticism to the Avant-Garde.* Cambridge: Harvard University Press, 1974.

Perloff, Marjorie. *Frank O'Hara: Poet Among Painters.* New York: George Braziller, 1977.

Poggioli, Renato. *The Theory of the Avant-Garde.* Cambridge: Harvard University Press, 1968.

Poirier, Richard. *Norman Mailer*. New York: The Viking Press, 1972.

Pound, Ezra. *ABC of Reading*. New York: New Directions, 1960.

_____. *Selected Poems*. New York: New Directions, 1957.

Pratt, William, ed. *The Imagist Poem*. New York: E. P. Dutton, 1963.

Reed, Ishmael. *Flight to Canada*. New York: Avon Books, 1977.

_____. *The Last Days of Louisiana Red*. New York: Avon Books, 1976.

_____. *Yellow Back Radio Broke-Down*. New York: Bantam Books, 1972.

Rexroth, Kenneth. *With Eye and Ear*. New York: Herder and Herder, 1970.

Rivers, Larry. "The Cedar Bar." *New York*, 5 November 1979, pp. 39–44.

Rosenberg, Harold. *The Tradition of the New*. New York: McGraw-Hill Book Co., 1965.

Rosenthal, M. L. "American Poetry Today." *Salmagundi*, nos. 22–23 (Spring-Summer 1973): 57–70.

_____. *The New Poets*. New York: Oxford University Press, 1967.

Sartre, Jean-Paul. *Anti-Semite and Jew*. New York: Grove Press, 1962.

_____. "Black Orpheus." In *The Black American Writer*, edited by C. W. E. Bigsby, 2: 5–40. Baltimore: Penguin Books, pp. 5–40.

Shange, Ntozake. *Nappy Edges*. New York: Bantam Books, 1980.

Smitherman, Geneva. *Black Language and Culture: Sounds of Soul*. New York: Harper & Row, 1975.

_____. *Talkin and Testifyin*. Boston: Houghton Mifflin Co., 1977.

Sollors, Werner. *Amiri Baraka/LeRoi Jones: The Quest for a "Populist Modernism."* New York: Columbia University Press, 1978.

Sutton, Walter. *American Free Verse*. New York: New Directions, 1973.

Tytell, John. *Naked Angels: The Lives and Literature of the Beat Generation*. New York: McGraw-Hill Book Co., 1976.

von Hallberg, Robert. *Charles Olson: The Scholar's Art*. Cambridge: Harvard University Press, 1978.

Whitman, Walt. *Leaves of Grass and Selected Prose*. Edited by John Kouwenhoven. New York: The Modern Library, 1950.

Williams, Martin. *The Jazz Tradition*. New York: New American Library, 1971.

Williams, William Carlos. *Pictures from Brueghel and Other Poems*. New York: New Directions, 1962.

_____. *Paterson*. New York: New Directions, 1963.

Woolf, Virginia. *The Death of the Moth and Other Essays*. New York: Harcourt, Brace and Jovanovich, 1974.

Zweig, Paul. "The New Surrealism." *Salmagundi* nos. 22–23 (Spring-Summer 1973): 269–84.

Index

172